COUNTLESS

A reflection on some of the countless miracles
of God at work through the ministry
of Sherwood Christian Rehab Centre.

by

Honi Reifler

NENGE BOOKS, Australia

COUNTLESS
by Honi Reifler

Copyright © 2017 Honi Reifler

All rights reserved.

This book or parts thereof may not be reproduced in any form, stored in a retreival system, or transmitted in any form by any means - electronic. mechanical, photocopy, recording or otherwise - without prior written permission of the publisher, in accordance with copyright laws, except in the case of brief quotations used in reviews, sermons or similar public media, with acknowledgement.

Cover art by Honi Reifler.
Cover background - Shutterstock.
Layout and desktop by NENGE BOOKS.
Published by NENGE BOOKS, Australia, December 2017
ABN 26809396184
nengebooks1@gmail.com

Revision 1, July 2018

Scripture quotations marked (NIV) are taken from the Holy Bible, New International Version®, NIV®. Copyright © 1973, 1978, 1984, 2011 by Biblica, Inc.™ Used by permission of Zondervan. All rights reserved worldwide. www.zondervan.com The "NIV" and "New International Version" are trademarks registered in the United States Patent and Trademark Office by Biblica, Inc.™
Scripture quotations marked (NKJV) taken from the New King James Version®. Copyright © 1982 by Thomas Nelson. Used by permission. All rights reserved.

NENGE BOOKS specializes in publishing small quantity runs of quality books using cost effective print-on-demand technology, and welcomes enquiries to assist in publishing biographies and other publications in both print and ebook form.

ISBN 978-0-6480675-3-5
Also available as an ebook ISBN 978-0-6480675-4-2

Dedicated

to the faithful staff who have served,

the seekers who have entrusted
themselves to us,

and the generous donors who have
enabled this work to flourish.

Contents

PREFACE	7
INTRODUCTION	9
1. REAL, REAL ESTATE	13
2. DEMONIC MANIFESTATIONS	21
3. UNEXPECTED MEETING OF BELIEVERS	28
4. FOOD – MULTIPLE BLESSINGS	33
5. DIVINE INSIGHT	38
6. MONEY! MONEY! MONEY! – GOD'$ INTERE$T	43
7. WHETHER THE WEATHER	49
8. MOBILE MISSION MAINTENANCE	55
9. PERSONAL ATTACKS	86
10. AUDACIOUSNESS	90
11. ACCIDENTS HAPPEN	95
12. MECHANICAL MIRACLES	101
13. ANGELS – AWARES AND UNAWARES	106
14. SHERWOOD GLEN	111
15. ANIMAL ANTICS	129
16. DANGER	135
17. HEAL THE SICK – RAISE THE DEAD	142
18. REVELATIONS TO UNBELIEVERS	153
19. BABIES - A LABOUR OF LOVE	156
20. OF DEATH AND DYING	166
21. WHAT'S NEXT?	174
WHAT IS SHERWOOD REHAB CENTRE?	182

PREFACE

This year, 2017, has been a big one for me! I farewelled my precious mother in July and welcomed our 18th grand-child in October, Honi Blossom. We celebrated our eldest son's 40th birthday, and I absolutely neglected my garden to write two books.

"Countless" is a collection of some of the God-incidents we have experienced: Far too many, too specific and too soul-inspiring to be simply shrugged off as co-incidences.

The other book is an illustrated children's book, part fact and part fiction. The Wanjidi Stories began as camp-fire yarns and grew into tales of kid's adventures at Sherwood over almost 100 years.

The Kemsley's capable leadership at Sherwood has enabled me time to stay home and write. Other staff have graciously shared the Sherwood work-load so my attention could be focused, my soul could be stirred and my pen could record the stories.

Georgie Quarmby deciphered my hand-written pages and typed them into an electronic format.

My three wonderful proof-readers have scanned and corrected the raw manuscript. Thank you Vonette Chad, Dulcie Reeves and Ruth Walker. Your diligence and encouragement have been greatly appreciated.

I thank my "neglected" husband for his patience and my inspiring children who encouraged me to write. Now that the books are completed I can once again enjoy lots of time with my grandchildren and lots of other God-given "littlies", rather than being pre-occupied.

One of the most hard-done-by characters recorded in the Bible, Job, was counselled with these wise words (in Job 5:8-9, NIV)

"But if I were you, I would appeal to God;

I would lay my cause before him.

He performs wonders that cannot be fathomed,

miracles that cannot be counted."

Honi Reifler
Sherwood Cliffs
November 2017

Mick - one of Honi's lovable rogues who epitiomises the joy of being part of a Sherwood seeker's journey in life.

INTRODUCTION

The wild-eyed young man looked up suspiciously as we stepped out of our car. In the flickering light of his campfire we introduced ourselves and he sullenly mumbled, "Who sent you?"

Squatting down next to the fire, JP casually replied, "God did!"

Disbelief, then anger flooded this dishevelled man's body. Immediately, he jumped to his feet and beat his fists on the roof of his car.

"Why? Why now?" he screamed at the dark night as his frustrated tirade continued. Finally, with emotions spent he slumped down onto the ground and began to heave with sobs. As the gentle waves washed onto the shore and a cool breeze stirred the surrounding bush, we listened to George's gut-wrenching story. He had tracked his wife from Victoria to Coffs Harbour and he was planning to kill her, and her lover, that very night. He was armed for the task and was just finishing cooking his meal when we arrived.

This was a God-orchestrated incident – not just a coincidence. George's devout Catholic mother in Victoria was praying for her disturbed son. JP happened to notice a car hidden in the coastal scrub when he was working that afternoon and he felt prompted to investigate. Although it was close to midnight when we arrived, we were an answer to a desperate mother's prayer and the timing was perfect.

George was just one of many people to whom we were Divinely led. But after the comfort, counsel and introduction to Jesus, what happens to disturbed folk? Although we were only in our early 20's and very young in our own relationship with God, He answered our prayers for wisdom in a mighty way. Whether it was a dream, a thought, a feeling or a vision, JP and I received the same calling. *"We were to set up a place, where people like George could have time to grow mentally, physically and spiritually."* The same leading, to two separate individuals! With the impulsiveness of youth we wanted it to happen now! But God, in His wisdom, knew that we needed to be prepared for the task.

That preparation took almost seven years, from the time of the vision until its fulfilment.

After marrying in early 1972 we moved to Western Australia and worked amongst the Aboriginal folk while I studied at University. Although we loved the people and threw our heart and soul into the city work, we knew that this was our training ground – the stepping-stones to something more. That 'something more' became Sherwood Cliffs, a place where people have drawn aside now for forty years, taking the time and receiving the support needed to heal and grow.

At Sherwood we have chosen to follow God's plans for us – to live by faith. This means that we are totally dependent on God to restore the broken lives of the addicts who come for help, to bring fellow workers in to share the vision as well as the 'blood, sweat and tears' of the ministry. Also, we are totally dependent on God for the financial wherewithal to raise up and operate the place.

"Running a rehab without secured Government funding or promised philanthropic investment is sheer madness," are the words we have had spoken over our lives on many occasions. We have no salary, have diminished our potential earning capacity, have committed career-advancement suicide, have no provision for sickness and/or accident insurance, and yet we have a deep peace. Not a foolhardy, head-in-the-sand type of peace! Not an airy-fairy type of peace! It's Jesus' peace, from the Prince of Peace.

God spoke into our lives – He gave us a mandate – a *God-date* – that if we were willing to run Sherwood His way, then He was willing to meet all of our needs. Our willingness was all that was required.

We thank God that this living by faith means we are totally "bankrupt" and, therefore, totally dependent on Him. All success, victory and provision do not come from our effort, but by His obvious intervention. If we had set up Sherwood with the "right" financial backing, the "right" endorsement and the "right" qualifications, then we never would have been totally dependent on God.

1971, JP & Honi's Engagement

Somebody once dubbed us as *"CLIFF-HANGERS IN THE LAST RESORT"*. Trawling through forty years of diaries, newsletters and memories, I realise how true this appellation is. It isn't blind faith that motivates us, but with eyes wide open and focused on Jesus, we are suspended over the unknown, the impossible, the ridiculous and the frightening – secure in the assurance of His presence.

COUNTLESS

As you read this book, a compilation of some of the countless miracles we have experienced, may you be encouraged, challenged, and even motivated to place your hand in the hand of Jesus. Desperate situations require definite choices. Knowing Jesus means that we can make the choice to choose Him. If you are willing, it's game on! Let the fun and faith begin!

1978 - The Pioneers

Chapter One

REAL, REAL ESTATE

1973

During our first year in Perth I started my Occupational Therapy studies and JP worked with youth for an Aboriginal Church. We rented an old duplex close to the city centre where I was the only Australian born resident in the street. At 10 pm when the wine saloon closed, the revellers passed our door on their way to the nightclub. Then in the morning, many who were unable to make it home could be found camped under the big trees in the park around the corner. Brothels and refuges abounded in this area. This was an ideal location for ministry.

Christmas 1973 God enabled us to make the hair-raising student flight to Europe, to meet JP's parents in Switzerland. On our return we looked for a big house to rent, but in a quieter location. One day JP felt that God wanted us to buy a house and He even gave him a vision of the place. This seemed ridiculous as we had a sum total of $60 in savings and we knew that our time in the city was limited because of the previous vision for a rehab farm. However, when he saw the exact house in Rivervale he approached the owners and discussed its purchase. The owners reduced the price from $18,000 to $16,000 and a Christian friend loaned us the money for the deposit.

Our bank manager tried to intimidate JP saying, "Young man, get your priorities right! Go out and work for money. Don't waste the best years of your life on the Aborigines."

This advice was not heeded, as we knew that God had a greater purpose for us than just "feathering our own nest."

After looking around at other options than the bank, we arranged a three-year bridging loan through a finance company. Their repayments were $48 a week and JP's wage from the Baptist Aboriginal Missions was $28 per week.

With the excitement of youth and the expectation of faith in a faithful God we moved into our five bedroom suburban home. After about three weeks we had a knock on the front door. Representatives from the finance company stood there and said, "Mr Bell, we're here to talk to you about the people who want to buy your home. They don't earn enough money to pay back a loan so we don't recommend that you sell to them."

With a glint in his eye and a spring in his step, JP ushered the visitors into the kitchen. Over a coffee, JP revealed that he wasn't Mr Bell, but the new owner of the house. "We have already moved in," he said excitedly, "and someone in your company has approved our loan. All the legal documents are signed and we have made our first payment."

The visitors looked worried at this news. "You need to go back to your office and find out what's going on," JP stated confidently as he saw the confused men to the door.

Over the next three years this house was a great place for ministry. The bedrooms were occupied by students, apprentices, and other young people making a start in the city. The large lounge room held up to 80 teenagers every Friday night for youth group and we even hosted a wedding reception in the spacious back yard.

Every month JP would proudly go into the finance company waving a cheque in his hand. "Look what God's done again. He's met the repayment!" he would tell all and sundry.

For three years we paid the eleven percent interest on the bridging finance for the house. But not one dollar was paid off the principle. Because we had no direction from God to move, we negotiated a one year extension on the bridging finance at twelve percent interest.

On a trip back to Coffs Harbour in 1977 we knew that the time was drawing closer to make the move to fulfilling the vision for a rehab farm.

1977

JP did his usual round of real estate offices to enquire if there was a suitable property to meet the vision requirements.

"We are looking for an isolated, disused farm, with permanent water and having one entrance," JP explained.

"Who's the WE?" the polite real estate agent enquired.

"God and I," JP excitedly replied. The patient agent humoured him along, extracting more details about the required land. After learning that JP's parents were visiting from Switzerland, he quizzically asked, "And how much money are you willing to spend?"

"Oh, money is no object! My Father's a millionaire!" JP confidently assured him.

The condescension then turned to genuine interest. JP was referring to his Heavenly Father, but the agent probably surmised that this "wayward" son was being financed by his parents, to stay well away.

"Well actually, I was having a beer in the pub last night with a bloke who told me to sell his property," the agent mused. "It sounds exactly what you want – out the back of Glenreagh – an old dairy farm." But then he continued a bit concerned, "The bloke was a bit under the weather. In the cold light of dawn, I don't know if he really does want to sell."

On our first inspection of the property we both instantaneously felt that this was it! This was the fulfilment of the vision given in 1971! Over the next ten days we walked on the land many times, sought Godly advice and human wisdom, and prayed continually.

Just as Gideon placed a fleece out before the Lord to discern His will, we did the same. Our "fleece" was to be the miraculous provision of the deposit for the farm by the date set by the real estate agent.

One thousand dollars was required within a month – by the 6th May. We asked God to use the amount and the timing of the deposit to confirm whether this was truly His place for us. On the long drive back to Perth, we prayed that the money would come miraculously – no "beg, borrow or steal", no manipulation, no solicitation, no bank loans. Only God was to know of our need.

On Monday 2nd May an old lady rang to say that God had spoken to her in her early morning devotions and that she should give us $500.

"What do you want it for?" she enquired.

"I can't tell you at the moment," JP replied.

"Well is it enough?" she asked.

"No, it's not. But if God doesn't supply the rest then we'll return your money, because you must have your wires crossed from Heaven," he confidently replied.

As the days drew closer to the deadline, we continued to pray fervently for God's will to be done. On the final day we had morning tea with an elderly couple in a retirement village. When we were leaving they pressed an envelope into my hands.

"Just a little something – use it for the coming baby or for whatever you have need," they said. As we were driving home up the highway I opened the envelope and gasped in amazement at a cheque for $500.

"You now have six months to pay the balance of $14,000," the real estate agent in Coffs Harbour said when he received the deposit.

We put our house on the market and gave the Aboriginal Church six months' notice of our departure. In the midst of the excitement and fear over the future, our first child, Luke, was born in mid-August.

In the last week of that six-month period, the house sold. Although we hadn't paid anything off the actual loan, only the interest on the bridging finance, we made $15,000 on the sale.

Property prices had inflated during the 3½ years that we had the house and now, miraculously, we could pay cash for the farm at Glenreagh.

1978

The only accommodation was a caravan and an old school bus and JP was frustrated with cramped living conditions. His prayer was answered when he responded to a dream about railway carriages.

"You stay here and pray," he excitedly said one morning. "I'm off to Grafton to the railway station."

The bemused stationmaster scratched his head after JP related his story of the vision for a rehab, the land at Glenreagh and his dream.

"I've been with the railways for 30 years and I've never sold a carriage yet. Only tickets for the train!" he said.

JP leaned over his desk, looked him straight in the eyes and said, "Look, does God lie? God told me last night that we were getting railway carriages..." excitedly thumping the desk, "And we are getting railway carriages!"

The stationmaster then rang a colleague in Sydney and thrust the phone at JP saying, "Tell him what you have told me!"

Half way into the story JP was halted with, "That's enough! How many carriages do you want?"

Stumped by this response, JP blurted out, "Half a dozen!"

"Righto then! The first two will arrive at Glenreagh Station in two weeks and they'll cost you $100 each!"

By the time they arrived, foundations were prepared and a truck and crane were organized. Embarrassingly, we didn't have the $200. Before we could plead our case or present a plausible delaying tactic the local stationmaster thrust a piece of paper at us.

In a confused voice he spluttered, "I've never seen anything like this before." The note said: "FIRST TWO CARRIAGES FREE OF CHARGE – TO GET THE GOOD WORK STARTED".

Six louvered vans were gradually being converted into housing when our Pastor, Don Kemsley, visited and said that he had received a phone call asking if "that funny pastor in the bush still wants railway carriages?" Two passenger wagons were available, but they would cost $150 each, and must be removed in one week.

"Tell him to ring me at Clyde Wagon Works by Friday if he wants them!"

Our heads went into overdrive as we contemplated the potential of 20 metre, metal, weatherproof carriages with real glass windows and proper doors. All week we prayed for the money, but nothing came.

On Friday JP dejectedly asked Don if he could use the church phone to decline the offer (Sherwood had no phones). "Before you ring I think you had better open this envelope first," Don said as he placed his hand onto JP's arm.

JP hooted in excitement when he counted out $300.

"A young couple, new to Coffs, came to Bible Study on Wednesday night for the first time," Don said. "They felt so touched by our prayers for Sherwood that they returned the next morning with this envelope. They told me that it is the tithing of their savings for a house deposit and it is for accommodation at Sherwood."

Twenty metre, 25 tonne passenger wagons are certainly a different proposition to move than 2½ tonne, 6½ metre long goods vans. Within days of our purchase, the enormous carriages had been delivered to the Coffs Harbour railway station.

Memories might fade about the moving of the carriages, but the whole exercise was captured on movie film. There were narrow bridges to negotiate, dirt roads, sharp bends, steep gullies, pouring rain, accompanying cranes, frustrated truck drivers and fading light to contend with. But finally both carriages were safely situated, to eventually create the main building on the rehab.

1979

In order to turn all the carriages and wagons into proper homes, building materials were required. We prayed about this need and a big, old, deserted house in Glenreagh came to mind. As we stayed in the car to pray JP approached the owner. The owner sat high on his horse, arms folded, face stern, thinking about the proposition. Minutes ticked by, JP shuffled his feet, kept talking and held onto the horse's reins. Finally the house owner replied, "You've caught me on the right day. I feel generous. You can have the old house for nothing!"

Over the years we have demolished churches, shopping centres, factories, clubhouses, restaurants and homes. All the building materials have been painstakingly removed, restored and used to construct the many houses and sheds at Sherwood Cliffs.

Broken lives have also been reconstructed during the restoration process. Interestingly, God has blessed us with all new building materials for the construction of Sherwood Glen. Now that properly registered demolition companies dominate the market, and strict occupational health and safety laws have come into existence, God provides in other ways to meet our needs and to witness to the world of His loving involvement.

Chapter Two

DEMONIC MANIFESTATIONS

Growing up in a stable, educated, God-fearing family, I was taught from an early age that there were no such things as ghosts. Dark night trips to the outside toilet were scary. "The bogey man won't get me," I chanted, "and there's no such thing as ghosts!" The fear was faced nightly, so I adopted the usual Western attitude to the demonic: It doesn't exist!

In preparation for Sherwood, God used our time in Western Australia amongst the Aboriginal people to shatter this belief. We learned that Satan is alive and well on planet earth. He is mighty! But God is almighty! The sacrificial death of God's Son broke the power of Satan so we don't have to live in the bondage of fear and the portent of Hell. As God's adopted children we are free.

1976

In his role as Pastor of the Nyoongar Church, and being employed by the Baptist Aboriginal Mission, JP sought out people who were hurting. He visited hostels and hospitals, refuges and parks, camps and homes, prisons and pavements.

One day he brought home a very disturbed, drunken man who was almost paralysed with fear. He was sure that a 'feather foot' (*uragi*), an Aboriginal tribal executioner, was pursuing him, to kill him. In our safe, suburban home we settled the distraught man into bed. His fear had so exhausted him that he quickly fell asleep. Shortly afterwards we were awakened by his piercing hysterical screams. Quickly I pushed JP out of bed to sort out the problem.

"The 'feather-foot' was here," he gulped. "It was here!" The terrified man slowly calmed down as JP spoke gently to him and prayed over him.

JP crawled into the other bed so his presence would help to reassure the frightened man. No sooner had JP nodded off to sleep when the man began to scream again. He clambered up on the pillow and pressed his trembling body hard into the corner. Pointing to the foot of the bed, ashen faced and trembling, he screamed, "He's here!"

JP looked toward where he was pointing and saw something. There was a small glowing figure hovering over the bed. *It's only the moonlight shining through the window,* he thought as he sat up. When he looked toward the window he instantly realised that this wasn't true. The wide verandah didn't allow any moonlight to shine into the bedroom.

Now he too was frightened. As the man continued to shake and sob, pressed against the wall, JP saw the 'feather-foot' materialise. A supernatural light glowed above and around it.

With God-given wisdom and boldness JP raised his hand and shouted, "In the name of Jesus, I rebuke you!" The apparition disappeared!

Terrified, the man jumped out of bed, bolted out of our house and ran off up the street. We never saw him again or heard anything more about him.

We were affronted with the audacity of Satan to enter our home. But we were comforted and excited by the power of the blood of Jesus over evil.

1981

Two passenger wagons had been purchased from the NSW State Railways a few years before and now housed three bedrooms, a small dining room and a seekers' kitchen. We were thankful for this wonderful accommodation but were concerned about regularly reported strange phenomena in one of the carriages.

One night a Seeker, (B), was awakened by his bed shaking. By torchlight he couldn't see anything and he couldn't turn on the light, as the generator didn't produce power after 10 pm. Every time he switched off the torch, the bed would shake again. When he tried to lie down he felt himself being lifted up from the bed and being dropped back onto it.

"Help! Wake up!" B screamed as he burst into our house in the middle of the night. "Something weird is happening in my room!"

JP settled B down, prayed with him and suggested he be available for counselling. Over the next two days, Charlie and JP delved into B's past, exposing much unholy activity. B let Jesus deliver him from unclean spirits.

When B finally completed his rehab, his room was being prepared for a new seeker when a strange mark was noticed. A standard railway fixture mirror, screwed to the wall of the carriage had an upside down cross, etched into the back of the glass. It looked as though a fingertip had wiped the reflective paint of the mirror away.

After a fascinated, frightened inspection of the mirror we all joined JP in anointing each room with oil and calling on the cleansing power of Jesus to remove any evil presence. The mirror was smashed and burned and a piece of timber was used to cover the gap in the wall. Another Seeker, in an adjoining room, was frightened by the appearance of the upside down cross. Even though she saw the freeing effects of B's deliverance ministry, she did not want to face her own dark hidden secrets, so she chose to leave a few days later.

The strange phenomena and evil manifestations ceased for a few years.

1984

Night after night, a young Seeker, R, felt himself being grabbed and lifted from his bed. When he switched on his torch, no one was there! R became increasingly frightened and unable to sleep, but he refused to allow JP or Charlie to pray with him.

One Saturday afternoon Staff members met together to pray for R in his absence. Suddenly, screaming and yelling were heard from the seeker's area. As we rushed outside we were horrified to see R being propelled backwards as he tried to fight off an invisible attacker. R was flung off the verandah, over a metre high railing and onto the lawn.

Immediately, JP rebuked Satan in Jesus' name and the conflict ended. R lay on the grass terrified and gasping for breath. Around his throat were raised red marks from the choking. As we comforted R he pleaded to be delivered from this evil power and to give his life to Jesus.

R's father was visiting for the weekend and that night, when he was sleeping in his son's room, he woke to the terrifying realisation that he was being strangled. As he pulled the choking hands from his throat, he screamed out to God for help. Frightened by this ordeal, he rededicated his life to God.

1998

A regular precious visitor from W.A., 80-year-old Effie Duke, had astounded us with her incredible ability at scrabble. She had resoundingly won the game!

Just before 10 pm, I was washing up when Effie dropped two cups as she approached the sink. I spun around and was horrified to see the expression on her face. Effie was very pale, the muscles in her face had dropped, her tongue protruded and her eyes were dull and half closed. Quickly, I wrapped my arms around Effie to stop her from falling and just managed to understand her garbled plea for prayer. I beseeched Jesus to reach out and touch Effie with His healing power.

Then I felt constrained to rebuke the powers of darkness that were trying to destroy this precious saint. Immediately Effie stood straight, her face returned to normal and her speech began to clear. After a good night's sleep, Effie showed no ill effects and was able to continue sharing her miracle stories and blessing us with her cheerful presence.

2003

Normally, each year begins with a very unstable group of Seekers who take until about Easter to settle down and find peace from their restlessness and determination to do rehab. However, this year the group was different. Georgie summed it up well when she said, "They are fair dinkum spiritually."

Many miraculous answers to prayer were experienced which encouraged their resolve – one was concerning a tattoo. Most seekers have tattoos. Some have been crudely done when under the influence of drugs, some were done in jail with limited equipment and some are amazing works of art.

One man had a horrific, demonic tattoo on his arm, which haunted him. It was a sign of the old life, which he desperately wanted to leave behind. Laser removal of tattoos is very expensive and was not an option at that time. We encouraged him to pray about his problem, as God loves to bless His people. I also told him about an incredible answer to my prayer regarding a tattoo.

Not long before our daughter, Chantal, was to be married to Colin, we ran into a young man in Coffs one Saturday afternoon. We had known him since he was a child and when we went to greet him with a hug, he stepped back from us.

In explanation he carefully removed his lightweight shirt and said that he had just stepped out of the tattoo parlour after a 3-hour inking. Covering his bicep was a perfect portrait of our daughter Chantal! We had always known that he was keen on her, but we thought that this tattoo was very inappropriate, considering her pending marriage to someone else! After we went on our way, we rebuked the tattooed image and asked Jesus to overrule the situation.

A few weeks later we met the young man again and he hesitantly showed us his arm. "I don't know what is happening. And neither does my tattooist," he sadly said. "I've never had it happen before!" To our amazement, where there had been a clear image of our daughter, now there was an indefinable smudge of coloured ink under his skin. Chantal's portrait was gone!

Over a coffee we explained to the young man about our concerns for the inappropriateness of the tattoo and how we had prayed about it. We assured him that his botched tattoo was an answer to our prayer and a sign for him that God was still reaching out to him in love. After a stunned realisation, he said that his tattooist had offered to re-ink the image as he considered it must have been from his poor workmanship. "I think that I'll get him to do something else then," the young man said. "I won't get him to do Chantal again."

On hearing this story, the seeker with the grotesque, demonic tattoo asked God to remove it. Although most of his body was decorated with ink from years of being tattooed, the offending tattoo started to change. At first the clear outline started to fade, then the image began to blur. Over weeks it became indecipherable, until finally all that was left were three small lines. "Those remaining lines remind me of the Trinity," the Seeker happily said as he proudly showed everyone his answer to prayer.

2010

In the book of Job there are two references to God putting a hedge around a person (1:10 and 3:23).

A young man, who spent only two weeks in rehab, desperately needed this hedging about so we covenanted to pray for him. During his high schooling he and his four friends tormented a fellow student who was into witchcraft. Their mockery caused her to retaliate with a curse on them. They laughed at her response, but the one who later became a Sherwood seeker pinpointed this event as the start of all his troubles.

As JP asked him to retrace his past, he said that from that time on he changed from being easy going to being overwhelmed with uncontrollable rages. Drug abuse followed and trouble with the law eventuated. It surprised him to see any significance in what he had always thought of as a meaningless gesture – a curse. Quietly he said that his other four friends had all died in tragic circumstances in the intervening years.

One Sunday at the beach, the seeker had a violent outburst and stormed off. "I want to be free of anger and drugs," he ranted. "But, I don't want to do it your way – with God and reading the Bible."

Although he refused to return to Sherwood, we felt a strong desire to cover him in prayer, to pray against the spirit of destruction, and that his eyes would be opened to the truth.

Chapter Three

UNEXPECTED MEETING OF BELIEVERS

1972

We married in February and headed west in our 36 horsepower Volkswagen Kombi bus. Although we had been given a vision for a place of refuge and restoration while in Coffs Harbour, we knew that we needed to be prepared for the task.

Along the way we prayed for cars to break down. There was no way that our little old Kombi could keep up with the fast moving traffic so we prayed that they would come to a standstill. Then JP, as a mechanic would come to their rescue while I made the stranded motorists a cup of tea. We could then share with our "frazzled subjects" the wonderful news about Jesus. Many interesting conversations ensued and many times it was obvious that this interruption was a God-incident for them.

Halfway across the country we parked for the night in a windswept salt marsh on Spencer Gulf in South Australia. Our bright orange Kombi, decorated with purple flowery curtains and Jesus stickers, stuck out in this stark location. No sooner had I begun preparing the evening meal when a police car cruised towards us. *Oh no, we're in trouble for illegal parking*, I thought.

The policeman leaned out of his window and shouted, "Follow me!" As we drove into the Police Station yard we prayed for the money to pay the possible fine.

The policeman walked towards us "quivering hippies", extended his hand and happily said, "Welcome to Port Wakefield! I saw your vehicle and read your signs earlier in the day when you were shopping in town. My wife and I are really missing Christian fellowship since moving to this posting. So, welcome!"

His wife and little children eagerly joined us from the police residence next to the station. That evening we enjoyed great fellowship, warm company and a delicious meal. God certainly has a big family and we share a common bloodline – the blood of Jesus Christ.

Before our departure the next morning we were blessed with fresh meat. They insisted that we catch and kill some of their chickens and ducks to help us on our journey.

1995

A young couple with a long history of drug abuse was desperate to come to Sherwood, but there was no suitable accommodation for a family.

Mission Mobile Maintenance (MMM) had almost finished a demountable building by installing a kitchen, but the plumbing was not connected. Our answer to prayer was 50kms away and God was on the job.

A banana farmer had a sudden thought that he should send some bananas out to Sherwood. Being busy at the time he pushed the thought aside. But each day a little voice persisted with the thought, *Send bananas!* Finally, first thing Monday morning he cut half a dozen bunches, in preparation, before wanting to ring JP to tell him to come and pick them up.

"Relief!" he said to himself. But then the "voice" said, *"Take the fruit to Sherwood!"* After delivering the welcome fruit and having morning tea, JP took him for a walk around.

We have a young family wanting to come, but our accommodation is full – except for a demountable that will be ready once the plumbing is done," JP said. Suddenly it all became clear to the man. "That's why God called me out to Sherwood Cliffs," he said to JP. "I'm a licenced plumber, even though I'm no longer in the building industry. God brought me out here to do this job!"

By the end of the following week the demountable was ready and the family moved in.

2011

After two agitated weeks in rehab, a young seeker woman demanded to leave. The myriad of excuses sounded rational to her, but the unacknowledged reason was that drugs were calling – loudly and cruelly. My heart grieved when I dropped her in Coffs Harbour. I grieved for the wasted potential, the dangers of her lifestyle, the bereft husband and her vulnerable children.

During the next month, we all covered the woman in prayer and rejoiced when she asked to come back. She missed the Tuesday train to return to Sherwood. *Were they real reasons or hollow excuses? Would this little delay be enough to derail the resolve to return to rehab?* we wondered.

On Wednesday she left Wollongong at 4 am and connected with the north coast train in Sydney. Georgie waited in Coffs, after the weekly food shopping, to meet her at 4 pm. However, a rail fatality at Kempsey stopped the train and passengers could not alight for two hours (hell for smokers!).

But God had a "ministering angel" on board the train who felt drawn to this obviously distressed woman. As they sat together, Liarne shared about her relationship with Jesus and her contact with Sherwood over 15 years. Having been saved from a similar lifestyle, Learne was able to defuse the discouragement that threatened to overwhelm.

Finally four hours later, Georgie warmly greeted the returning seeker and dropped the "ministering angel" off to her Coffs Harbour home.

2012

(This little "ministering angel" has blonde hair, blue eyes and was two years old at the time).

Supermarkets, with their bright lights, busy shoppers and towering shelves can be places of sensory overload for the vulnerable. As I unloaded my trolley onto the checkout area, my accompanying Seeker bravely decided to duck back up the aisles to find the zip-lock plastic bags (the last item on the list).

Suddenly panic overwhelmed her. She couldn't find me! Just before she was about to "lose the plot" and have a giant "meltdown" she spotted a cute little girl sitting in a shopping trolley. When Mimi smiled at her, she grabbed hold of the handles of the trolley for 'grim death'.

"Mimi! Mimi!" was all the distraught Seeker could say – as Mimi kept smiling and chatting to her.

Mimi's confused father, Shaun, wondered who this obviously anxious woman was – and how she knew his daughter. Unable to get a coherent response, he came to the conclusion that she must be from Sherwood, as his wife often visited Chantal to help out, and Mimi must have met her there. He then saw me at the checkout, trying to sort out my various orders and glancing anxiously around for my missing Seeker.

Although shaken by the experience, the Seeker managed to see God's tangible hand, in not only sending an ex-staff

(Shaun) but also a little "Mimi-angel" to distract her from her anxiety.

On our next trip to town an 'angel' wasn't necessary, as she had grown in confidence through the previous week's intervention.

Chapter Four

FOOD – MULTIPLE BLESSINGS

2012

The year began with a very sceptical group of seekers. They were sceptical about the very existence of God, and if He was there, they were sceptical about His personal interest in them.

It was my turn to read the morning devotions and it was from John 6:1-4 where Jesus fed the 5,000 hungry men. Amidst the atmosphere of scepticism, this was no time for a theological abstraction, but rather, for a personal illustration. Having experienced many of God's miraculous blessings of food, I related three relevant incidents. Devotions ended with a query about my sanity and credibility – but, God had the last laugh!

The following Saturday, evening numbers at the barbecue exceeded Georgie's expectations. A desperate prayer to "multiply the food" was shot up to Heaven – within the earshot of the two biggest sceptics. As everyone sat around the fire to eat, it was obvious that all 53 plates were full of food!

The next day the esky was accidentally forgotten to be packed into the bus. All we had brought was a watermelon! Thankfully, some visitors who had joined us at the picnic after church, had brought along 2 barbecue chooks, 4 bread rolls,

2 small salads and 2 packets of hot chips! God miraculously blessed this food and 28 people were fed – fully!

The following Wednesday's devotions began with a begrudging acknowledgement of the miracles by the sceptics. A subtle change in attitude could be discerned. That day's reading was from John 10:38 and said, *"...even though you do not believe me, believe the miracles, that you may know and understand that the Father is in me, and I am in the Father."* (NIV)

1999

A similar incident had occurred at another barbecue in 1999 when numbers swelled unexpectedly. Twenty five cobs of corn were cut in half – but there were 84 people to feed.

"Help Lord, we need a miracle!" we prayed as we smilingly served each person. When everyone was served and the pot was empty, I did the calculations. Three people didn't want corn but 81 took a piece – Hallelujah!

2002

Feeding unexpected visitors is not a problem with certain meals – a bit of extra water in the soup, a few more vegetables in the stew, stretching out the stroganoff, spinning out the salad... But with chicken legs, it's a different matter! Sandy had carefully counted out the chicken legs – 3 for men, 2 for women and teenagers, and 1 for the younger children.

At 5 pm a family of four dropped in to visit and were, naturally, invited to join us for our evening meal at 6 pm. There was no time to thaw, marinate and cook any more chicken legs, so Sandy prayed for God to multiply the meal.

Meanwhile, another drama was unfolding. Two young men were returning from work along Sherwood Creek Road when their vehicle got two flat tyres. Because their spare tyre was already flat, they slowly drove up to the nearest farm, Sherwood Cliffs, to ring for help.

The NRMA couldn't come for another hour so the young men were invited to join us for dinner. When they entered the dining room they were amazed at the numbers, the noise and the high spirits.

Sandy shot up another quick prayer and kept serving the meal. Jokingly, the men were told that we needed a 'loaves and fishes' style miracle to feed the increased number, particularly with the pre-counted chicken legs.

They enjoyed the meal and joined in with the conversation, but were uncomfortable in the setting, especially when it was noted that there were not only enough chicken legs for all, but some for seconds as well.

2005

Carolyn was unpacking the food shopping when she discovered that the eight lettuces ordered had not been included. As the following day was a public holiday and a picnic was planned, it was very inconvenient not to be able to have a lettuce-based salad in such hot weather.

Jake's fresh vegies

Later that evening, a couple from Nowra (700 kms south) arrived with a new seeker...and a box of lettuce. June said that she had felt prompted to bring the lettuce so had picked them from her garden while it was still dark, early in the morning. We celebrated Australia Day at the beach with a barbecue and a large lettuce salad.

2007

Surprise visitors caused the cooks some consternation, as the 30 lamb chops had to now feed 39 people. Mathematically, it was impossible, so saying grace before the meal was an expression of desperation. God heard – after all, He's had some practice at this type of miracle and this was hardly 5000 mouths to feed!

Every plate was allocated a lamb chop and there were still 8 chops left over for seconds. Praise Him!

2008

One Wednesday, on my way home from Coffs Harbour, after doing the weekly food shop, I realised that I hadn't ordered steak from the butcher. When a visiting group comes to Sherwood for a pre-booked lunch we always serve a barbecue of steak and salad. A group was booked in for the following day!

To my surprise, as I unpacked the groceries, I discovered that the butcher had inadvertently given me 60 steaks – instead of the 60 lamb shops which I had ordered for normal meals. I just knew that this was no mistake!

The next day I took the visiting group on a walk-and-talk around Sherwood. We stopped in on the busy Mobile Mission Maintenance ladies who had set up a curtain-making workshop in the school's kitchen.

"We are a faith work," Gwen said in reply to a question about financial remuneration. "We give of our time and talents freely, and God enables us to meet our needs." I, too, had been telling the visitors about God's marvellous provisions to enable Sherwood to operate, but I knew that this was an unfathomable concept.

At lunchtime, the 16 visitors, 16 'MMMers', 36 'Sherwoodites' and two other visitors filed past the barbecue. Seventy people received a steak – when there were only 60 pieces available. Colin said that he shot up a quick prayer when he saw the numbers in this line compared to the number of steaks which he had cooked. No-one missed out!

What a wonderful opportunity I had, to share with the visitors that they were part of a miracle. This is what faith in our Lord Jesus is all about! This is how Sherwood and MMM operate! We do our best and then we leave the rest up to God.

The miracle of the steak met a temporal need, but we pray that it will have eternal consequence as spiritual eyes are opened.

Chapter Five

DIVINE INSIGHT

The Bible says, *"If any of you lacks wisdom he should ask God who gives generously..."* (James 1:5). Many times we stand on this promise when dealing with tricky situations and *gutter-smart* people.

1979

Because Sherwood is a residential rehab any changes of behaviour are quickly noticed. For a few days JP noticed that Hugh was acting strangely and it appeared that he was *high*.

Even after confrontation where Hugh proclaimed his innocence, the symptoms persisted. JP prayed for wisdom and he saw a picture of a tree near the water tank up on the cliff ledge. On the ground, near the tree, he saw a saucepan-sized rock covered in moss.

A little later, JP nonchalantly suggested that he and Hugh go for a bush walk up to the water tank.

"I don't want to go!" Hugh (not his real name) vehemently said.

"Oh yes, you're coming!" JP insisted.

As they climbed up to the tank Hugh became increasingly nervous and kept denying that he had ever been up that way before. JP stopped at the tree near the tank and pointed at a mossy rock.

"Pick up that rock," he stated

Ashen-faced Hugh answered, "Pick it up yourself!"

JP said again, "Pick it up!"

"No, there might be a snake under it," Hugh said as he tried to back away. JP took a firm hold on the front of Hugh's shirt and demanded, "Pick it up!"

Slowly Hugh complied. In a hollow underneath the rock was a plastic bag containing a tube of glue.

Denial was useless, so all Hugh could splutter was "How did you know? Did you follow me up here?"

"The Lord showed me where it was," JP quietly replied.

This incident, and other similar ones, shook up the seekers and showed us how much we could trust God to provide wisdom in any situation.

1983

Laughter is the best medicine in rehab as the following story shows.

The bright yellow moneybox pig had gone missing from the office when JP was called away. Kelly (not her real name) had been the only person close by so JP confronted her.

"Where is my phone pig?" he demanded. With all the practice of the pathological liar, Kelly replied, "I swear to God I know nothing about it!"

After applying a little pressure, Kelly pretended to be receiving a vision.

"I can see the pig lying under a bush, behind the shed," she dreamily said.

When she led JP to the spot, there was the pig, but it was empty. Kelly tried an innocent shrug of her shoulders, but JP demanded, "Get that money for me now!"

Realising that the game was up, Kelly went to her bedroom where all the money was secretly tucked inside four pairs of socks.

Attempting a wide-eyed innocent stare Kelly said, "Well, I don't know how it got there!"

1996

After seekers leave the programme we uphold them before God when we are prompted to pray. Certain people seem to be brought to mind more often than others. *Br...* was one of these!

Since leaving Sherwood five years previously, many of us had felt constrained to pray for him on many occasions. One day he rang to ask if he could stay for a few days on his way south to Melbourne. What a surprise!

In those intervening years *Br...* had been in and out of trouble with drugs, the occult and the law (including a lengthy jail sentence). At times he worried that he had become too bad for God. But even in those dark times he said that he felt God wanting to draw him back into the light.

When *Br...* visited, he asked if he could go into his old bedroom to look out of the back window. What he saw made him fall to his knees and cry and cry. He looked at a large boulder at the edge of the rainforest on which a native fig tree was growing. That tree, with its roots going down into and over the rock, had grown taller but it was not in a healthy state.

Weeds had grown all over the rock, so that the rock itself was barely visible. Vines were climbing into the tree and starting to strangle it.

Br... felt that this was a picture of his own life. Previously, the tenacious tree growing strongly in such a hard spot had encouraged him. Now, the ravages of weeds and vines compromised the tree's health and growth. He felt that

Jesus, as the Rock, was still there supporting and sustaining him, but because of sin, Jesus was barely visible and had to compete with the threatening invasion.

This divine insight prompted *Br...* to get his life right with God again. As he departed he promised that, "The next time I visit I'll clear the rock of all the weeds."

Sadly there wasn't a next time! *Br...* died a few years later but we have Jesus' promise that *"I will never blot out his name from the book of life but will acknowledge his name before my Father and his angels"* (Rev. 3:5, NIV).

1997

While taking the three teenagers to high school one Monday morning, JP glimpsed a man standing outside a motel. Immediately, he felt a strong urge that this man was in need. After dropping the children at school, 15 kms south of Coffs Harbour, JP headed back into town. The man had crossed over the Pacific Highway and was now hitchhiking north.

As soon as the man was in the car JP introduced himself and bluntly asked, "When are you going to do something about your drug problem?" After spluttering in surprise the man replied, "How strange. Someone talked to me the other day about Sherwood Cliffs and I wanted to contact you. I have been given a Bible and I have started reading it. Now you are here! I can see that something is going on."

That man has not made any further contact as JP encouraged him to, but God knows him by name and the 'HOUND OF HEAVEN' is in pursuit.

2013

As I was sitting on my verandah writing I received a very welcome phone call. After catching up on all the family news since they left Sherwood six years previously, the caller then told me about an interesting occurrence.

Her husband hadn't touched *hard* drugs since but he still "needed" alcohol daily. For one week he was awakened at 16 minutes past 3 every morning. When he complained to his wife, she replied that perhaps God was trying to get his attention. In frustration he grabbed a Bible and it fell open at John 3. Verse 16 jumped out at him!

Although this reminder of God's love through Jesus shook him, it didn't motivate change. However, as his wife said, God hasn't given up on him yet and it has given her a quiet confidence.

Chapter Six

MONEY! MONEY! MONEY! – GOD'$ INTERE$T

Early in our Christian lives we were both impressed with miraculous stories of God's provision for George Muller to meet the needs of 5,000 orphans in his care. Although this faithful man lived in the 1800's and on the other side of the world (England) we felt led to trust God also in the same manner. Philippians 4:6 was our guide, *"Do not be anxious about anything, but in everything by prayer and petition, with thanksgiving, present your requests to God."* (NIV)

For six years in Western Australia we had put our total trust in God to provide all of our needs: And He had poured out His miraculous provision. In 1977 as we were heading back to the eastern states to occupy the farm that God had miraculously provided, I was re-reading George Muller's story. Once again we were divinely inspired to continue to trust God in this new venture. It was to be a witness to an unbelieving world, and a doubting church, of His goodness, faithfulness and love. There were to be no bank loans, government handouts, soliciting or requested sponsorship. There was to be no "beg, borrow or steal". God alone was to be our provider.

1985

One day Sue returned home to Sherwood with a $47 donation from a lady in her Bible study group.

"God told me to give you this specific amount," the lady said. "So will you please tell me what it is meant for?"

That afternoon a bill for $297 arrived in the mail for fuel used by the trucks when demolishing two houses a few weeks previously. Continuing to open the mail there were two cheques – one for $200 and in another envelope $50. Added to the lady's $47, we had the exact money to pay the fuel bill.

1985

There was no electricity in the Sherwood valley when we arrived, so we produced power with a generator. Apart from this being costly it also created problems, with electrical fluctuations causing motors to burn out easily. As our numbers grew, so did the demands on the generator. However, a quote of $165,000 from the State electricity provider ruled out that option and sent us back to praying for a solution.

At that time we had a seeker who was an electrician. Brian had been in a horrific motorbike accident and his pain had been managed with morphine-based painkillers in the hospital. An addiction developed which was only satisfied with heroin after morphine was no longer prescribed. Brian's rehabilitation progressed well as he slowly replaced drugs with a growing awareness of Jesus. The greater replaced the lesser!

At the end of his six months, Brian was not confident to return to his trade so he asked if could stay on at Sherwood and re-wire the whole place to meet State standards. "If ever you are connected to the grid you will be ready," he said.

Shortly afterwards we were notified that State power was being brought into the valley as a rural developer had bought 1,000 acres and divided it into 10 blocks. Our two neighbours were now interested in connecting to mains power so the cost would be shared between 13 of us – if we were interested.

A contract was signed and $16,000 was due in three months. Brian's re-wiring encouraged us to believe that this was God's plan and so we prayed with great faith to our great God.

Six thousand dollars came in but the three-month period for total payment was fast approaching. Surely God would provide the remaining $10,000 in time.

One day a strange, old man drove in and demanded a guided tour. With his bare feet, baggy shorts and terry-towelling hat he held onto JP's arm for support as he was shown around.

"What's that?" he asked when he saw a power pole. "Why hasn't it got wires on it?"

By faith, JP had bought eight old power poles and had erected them with insulators he had found at the tip. "We're getting organised" JP replied.

"Organised for what?" the old man, Bob, asked.

"State power," JP answered.

"How much will that cost?" Bob demanded.

JP didn't want to tell this old man a specific figure as the Lord had told us to make our requests to Him – and not to people. So JP said, "The Lord will provide!"

With a glint in his eye, Bob steered JP back to our kitchen and demanded another cup of coffee.

"Pass me my bag," Bob said as he drank. Old newspapers, sandwiches and rubbish poured out all over the table until he reached thousands of dollars.

Bob turning the power on

"How much do you need for the power?" Bob asked again. Before JP could give an evasive answer, Bob said, "Well this obviously isn't enough and I don't want to be short of spending cash, so I'll be back tomorrow with a cheque."

JP was full of faith, but the rest of us were very doubtful about this eccentric looking visitor.

Bob returned the next day as promised. When JP returned home from his usual Friday shopping we could barely contain our excitement. Bob had left an Australian flag and a cheque for $10,000 – the exact amount needed to connect to State power and on the last day of the three-month contract period!

1990

In answer to my prayers for a babysitter to care for my children while I went to an Occupational Therapist's reunion in Perth, a sprightly 79-year-old Effie Duke stepped in. I really wanted to repay her for her kindness, but not knowing how, I asked God to do it for me.

On the morning of Effie's departure she was lightening her suitcases by giving me a shopping bag she had purchased at an opportunity shop some time before.

"The zipper on the top works," she said, "but the one at the side won't open."

With that, she tried the offending zipper and it slid open easily! To our absolute amazement, inside the pocket was a bundle of notes, secured with an old elastic band. I counted out $310 - $60 of which was in $2 notes that had been out of circulation for years.

Effie was flabbergasted! When she finally could speak, she said, "Thank you Lord – that will pay for my car registration." I also thanked God for blessing this faithful friend in a far greater way than I would have been able to do.

1989

On Wednesday we received a cheque for $1,000 and there was nothing specified for its use. We thanked God for this wonderful provision and asked Him to show us clearly the use He intended for the money. Sunday came and we barely made it home from Church. There was something drastically wrong with the motor in the bus. A visiting diesel mechanic stripped down the motor and discovered the problem. The spare parts cost $1027 and the bus was back on the road the following Sunday. What a wonderful God we have! He provided the money before we knew of our need, as well as the diesel mechanic to carry out the repairs!

2014

After seven years of service at Sherwood, the Kemsley family took three months off to do a road trip around Australia. One of their "God incident" experiences indelibly exposed their children to the goodness of God.

As they drove the long hot roads of northwest Australia, they stopped at a broken-down car to find a Swiss couple stranded with a split plastic radiator. Versatile and practical Colin temporarily solved their problem, by melting zip-ties and pouring the liquid plastic onto the split.

The Kemsleys then drove with the couple into the nearest town, (100kms away), where a replacement radiator was ordered. They were told that it would take three days to come up from Perth, so the Kemsleys spent those days exploring Ningaloo Reef while the Swiss couple stayed on in Exmouth.

When the Kemsleys returned, the radiator hadn't arrived, but the garage promised it would be there the next day. So the Kemsleys decided to stay an extra day to help their new friends. The caravan park cost $52 and they refused the offer of the Swiss couple to pay this expense.

After the successful replacement of the radiator, they farewelled their friends and headed south. A few hundred kilometres down the road the four bored, boisterous kids needed to run off some energy. They pulled over and followed a fisherman's track down to the inviting Indian Ocean. Colin stopped at something caught in a prickly spinifex bush. There, waiting for them, was a $50 note - old, battered and looking like it had been around the world a couple of times, but it was still cashable!

2015

While we were away in Switzerland Colin and Chantal started the mammoth task of de-cluttering Sherwood. Old vehicles and white goods were sold to the scrap metal dealers. When a payment of $1732 arrived Chantal planned to use it to re-organise the shed. However, the very next envelope opened contained a fuel bill for $1710. Reluctantly, Chantal realised that this was too much of a God-incidence to ignore and handed over the scrap metal cheque. She wondered how much the $20 would achieve in her reorganisation plans.

This is how she responded to the situation: *God is good all the time, it is us who often fail to see His generosity in each and every situation. We take it upon ourselves to claim the glory and the profit for the "work" we have done – rather than be in awe, filled with gratitude, for all that He has done. Praise God for that $22. Every cent is a gift and we are grateful for His faithful generosity toward His work at Sherwood.*

Chapter Seven

WHETHER THE WEATHER

Miraculous events that we have experienced are not because of our power to command Heaven but because our Saviour, Jesus Christ, delights to bless His people. Some of the following stories of weather events reflect this truth.

Acts 28:1-10 tells of Paul's shipwreck on Malta and how a poisonous snake bit him. He shook the snake off and into the fire and was unharmed. Selwyn Hughes in his daily devotional – *"Every Day With Jesus" (15th May 2017)* makes this comment:

"Had he (Paul) allowed a poisonous snake to bite him to prove Jesus' miraculous intervention and then survived, that would have given the Christian faith an unfortunate twist – the magical would have replaced the moral."

1985

The previous year a shopping centre in Coffs Harbour had been demolished and a large stockpile of building materials was ready for MMM's annual work party. Council had approved the plans for a machinery and storage shed, which would also provide a covered work area. The year had already been extremely wet with the annual rainfall received by May.

Charlie and a team of seekers had spent days filling potholes in the soggy Sherwood road with crushed sandstone to provide easier access for the twelve-tonne crane.

Russell and his offsiders had set upright railway lines into concrete. The MMM team had arrived and was ready and rearing to work.

"Do you really want us to send out the crane?" the anxious receptionist from the hire place said. "It's pouring in Coffs Harbour!"

"Yes, definitely," JP replied. "It's not raining out here. We need to start today, otherwise we won't get the job done within the two weeks of our work party's visit."

Preparations continued and the sky remained clear.

Once more the receptionist rang, worried about the weather conditions. Once again she was assured that we wanted to go ahead.

Charlie had been burdened to pray for a fine day and was really concerned about the deteriorating weather. Just as the crane arrived, dark curtains of rain started moving across the farm.

"John, we have to stop and pray," Charlie implored. "We'll pray at dinner time," JP offhandedly replied as he directed the crane toward the building site.

"No, now!" Charlie urgently insisted. "The rain is nearly here!"

Sensing Charlie's concern, JP called for everyone to *down tools*, stop the generator, and turn off the motors on the crane and other vehicles. With the impending rain beating its way up the paddock, every head was bowed as JP stretched out his arms toward the ominous sky.

"God, we rebuke the storm in Jesus' name!" he shouted.

Eyes that were closed in prayer, opened to witness an amazing sight. Miraculously, the rain sheet that had been heading directly towards them divided and swept around the stunned onlookers. Not one drop fell where the shed was to be built.

Quick, amazed utterances of "Praise the Lord" were shouted as the motors were switched back on. The crane began lifting the 15 metre wide roof trusses onto the railway-line uprights. Not a breath of wind disturbed the delicate alignment of truss and post as the men slipped bolts through

the prepared holes and then secured them with nuts.

Within two hours the trusses were all in place and the crane driver said, "The boss told me to charge you at last year's rates, and you don't have to pay for the travelling. That'll be ninety dollars, thanks," but he made no mention of the miracle of the storm's departure.

Our curiosity to know if he actually realised what had happened, was satisfied by my niece. A couple of days later, she was waiting for a train at the Coffs Harbour

railway station when she couldn't help but overhear a loud conversation between a group of workmen. One man was excitedly describing the events at Sherwood as he saw it from his position in the crane. "They must have God on their side," he concluded.

At evening devotions, when the frenetic activity of the initial construction stopped, great waves of praise to God arose from all at Sherwood. His obvious, miraculous intervention had parted the threatening storm.

1980

Every seven years God miraculously provides for us to visit Switzerland to reconnect with JP's family. Although we were excited about the impending trip and the new baby (Marcus) who would be born there, we were concerned about leaving Sherwood in its fledgling state.

The only staff were 17 year old Joanne Keast plus Charlie and Jean Quarmby who had just started in September of the previous year. They assured us *that when God calls, God equips*, and so they were willing to hold the fort, in His strength.

During our absence people came for counselling, potential seekers made enquiries however, nobody came to stay.

But an enemy far greater than a human sense of failure was at work – it was the cruel enemy, drought. The creek (through Sherwood) stopped flowing, dams dried up and the water tanks were soon empty.

Laboriously, empty drums were put onto the back of the land Cruiser and water was pumped out of the diminishing pools in Sherwood Creek. The four kilometre round trip ensured that farm animals and fruit trees were kept alive. Drinking water had to be brought in on any, and every, trip to Coffs Harbour.

Rather than feel inadequate Charlie, Jean and Joanne knew that the lack of seekers was God's doing in light of the staffing and water situation.

As soon as we arrived home, 550mls (22 inches) of rain fell in one week. The lack of water was over, and so was the seeker drought. Many, many people arrived for rehabilitation, including two teenage girls who continued their schooling by correspondence lessons. Another young seeker arrived and she was a wonderful help to me with Luke (2½) and baby Marcus.

1987

Australia is a *"land of droughts and flooding rains"* as Dorothea McKellar aptly described in her poem *"MY COUNTRY"*.

Charlie's weather records showed that only half the annual rainfall had been received since the previous year, and he was particularly burdened by the situation. Capitalising on the dry creek bed, we were loaned a bulldozer to build a new dam. As Chris steadily dug the dam, Charlie warned that we had only enough water remaining to supply Sherwood's needs for a further two weeks.

"Then we will have to close up, send the majority of people away and keep only a skeleton crew here to feed animals, tend gardens and answer phones," he warned. Even more fervent prayer petitioned God to have mercy on this dry, parched land.

Late one Friday afternoon, Chris put the finishing touches to the dam wall and considered leaving the dozer in the hole so he could complete the final tidying up of the banks the next day. Caution, experience and wisdom prompted him to drive the dozer out of the deep, dry hole.

We woke the next morning to the sound of heavy rain. With 300mm (12 inches) falling in the following two weeks, the new dam filled to capacity and so did the other dams and all the water tanks. We praised God for this timely, abundant provision of rain. But we also praised Chris for his ability to make a dam and for his wisdom to remove the borrowed dozer from the once dry hole!

2013

Charlie served His Lord faithfully at Sherwood for almost 30 years and he retired at 80 years of age. When he died in Sydney in 2013, many of us were able to go to the funeral.

A special memorial service was held at Sherwood a few weeks later. As 165 people gathered for the occasion, so did ominous storm clouds. People came from Coffs Harbour to north of Grafton, Woolgoolga to Nana Glen, and everyone spoke of the heavy rain that they had driven through. God, in His mercy, spared us from a wet evening, so we could enjoy an outdoor meal around a warm, open fire.

After it was all over, I wearily headed home rejoicing that so many people honoured this wonderful man. I was amazed to see the huge puddles of water on the road, just outside the Sherwood gate. God had once again held back the rain.

Chapter Eight

MOBILE MISSION MAINTENANCE

The accommodation at Sherwood began with an old school bus and a caravan. Then, miraculously we were able to purchase eight goods vans and two passenger wagons from the railways. Old houses in the district were demolished to add to the building supplies and a saw mill was set up to cut trees from the property. When the Lockwood family joined us in 1981 Russell (a licenced builder) pushed the building program ahead. However the needs were greater than one very diligent man could handle. Apart from using second hand materials and operating the sawmill, Russell also had to work with seekers whose lives were fragile and skills often minimal.

A lovely eighty-year-old man, Stan Goodwin, offered to help and he set about re-constructing the schoolhouse that had arrived the year before. Realising the large number of buildings eventually needed, he recommended that we apply to *Mobile Mission Maintenance* for help. This fledgling ministry had commenced in Victoria to help churches and other Christian organisations with their building and maintenance. We were absolutely delighted to learn that they would send a work party the following year.

So began a long association with this wonderful organisation and the many saints who willingly shared their skills, life experiences and wisdom with us. Truly they epitomise their motto – *Serving those who serve*.

1983

Stan's connections with MMM paved the way for an initial work party in late June.

Russell's plans for roofing over the two passenger carriages were approved by our local Council. We prayed for money to purchase building materials and $1,000 came in within two days so we were assured that God blessed this project.

Forty-eight tall, straight gum trees were cut down off the property, trimmed and de-barked for the pole structure. On either side of each carriage six poles were cemented into the ground but the 12 metre high central poles had to be placed in position with a crane.

Once the cement was dry and the uprights braced, the crane lifted the horizontal poles along the full length of each 20-metre carriage. Anxiously we watched the delicate manoeuvring of the heavy, long poles praying that a wind wouldn't spring up and blow the suspended poles about. While standing on scaffolding, the men aligned the pre-cut joints and then bolted the horizontal and vertical poles firmly together.

The Monier Company had been giving us tiles over the years, thanks to a Christian friend who worked for them. In an assortment of colours, 4,000 tiles had been stockpiled for this job with thousands of chipped and cracked tiles turned into road base. In late June, the inaugural MMM team arrived to work on the roof skeleton. To the rhythmic beating of hammers, the rafters braced the poles together. Under the proud gaze of his daughters, the team leader, Max Maddock, used his router to carve a message into the barge boards – *"UNLESS THE LORD BUILDS THE HOUSE THEY LABOUR IN VAIN WHO BUILD IT"*.

At this time a popular song of George Harrison's, *"My Sweet Lord,"* permeated the airwaves. So, when asked for a pithy slogan to write on the roof, I quickly replied, *"Jesus is Lord"*. I didn't want any *bhagwan* or *guru* to steal the truth

MMM Work Team

from Jesus – He is our Lord. With just the exact number of white tiles available, the clever tilers spelled the message across the new roof.

The MMM team's visit was exhilarating and encouraging for us, but it was also exhausting, as we had to maintain a stable environment for the seekers. The seekers were often fragile emotionally, felt rejected by the busyness, paranoid because of the visitors, and felt inadequate with all the amazing competency of the team. However, the intensity of the two weeks of MMM's work party helped them to face these fears and to grow stronger as they overcame these emotional responses.

1984

The previous year MMM constructed a roof over the two passenger wagons and the next year they returned to continue the work.

An unexpected and unsolicited gift for the job came from the *Coffs Harbour Lions Club*. This money purchased bricks for the end walls and flooring timber for the bottom storey of the building. A Christian bricklayer and his offsiders freely gave of their time to build the walls.

By faith we ordered a second truckload of cypress flooring for the top storey. Continually we thanked God that He would provide the $1,000 necessary to pay for the extra timber. On Monday the timber arrived, on Tuesday God provided the full payment through the sale of a donated diamond ring and on Thursday the first of the MMM team turned up.

Co-operative manpower lifted the heavy poles so that they could be winched up to form the weight bearing beams for the top storey. The MMM team laid the cypress flooring on both levels and built a connecting staircase.

At the end of a hard day's work, the evening meal and praise points were an opportunity to acknowledge the blessing of achievements amidst laughter – truly *"a merry heart does good like a medicine"*.

1985

Work didn't continue on the main building in 1985 because, at the end of the previous year, a shopping centre in Coffs Harbour was demolished and all the building materials were set aside for a large work shed. Therefore the MMM work party focused on the construction of this shed.

Roof trusses, iron, timber and glass were prepared and a site was levelled with a bulldozer. By the time MMM arrived the continual wet weather (the annual rainfall had already been received in five months) pushed ahead the need for an undercover work area. Once the basic structure was securely up, the original roofing from the shopping centre was used to clad the walls.

The amazing story of God's parting of the approaching storm front has been told in the chapter before.

New iron was then purchased for the roof of the shed from the sale of an old house. The house had been given for removal but it wasn't suitable to relocate to Sherwood, therefore it was sold, and the money used for bulldozer hire and new roofing iron.

God dealt with the weather and provided all the materials for the job. Because of MMM's generous presence we had no outstanding costs and we were blessed with a huge 18x15 metre shed – an ideal, dry work area.

1986

The new kitchen and dining room between the two passenger carriages were slowly taking shape but they still weren't usable. We were still cooking in the guard's room and eating in the rest of the carriage. When the temperatures soared in the tiny kitchen and the noise simultaneously soared in the dining area, we were encouraged by George Muller's wise words – *"The only way to learn great faith is to endure great trials"*.

MMM Work Team

However, a greater need for MMM's annual work party was to focus on completing the school house so that the children could move from the temporary classroom which they had occupied since school started in 1983. A single room schoolhouse, which was constructed early in the century, (and had closed in the 1970's), had been given to us from a Taree farmer. In order to transport it over 200kms it had been cut into 2-metre wide sections. Painstakingly over the years, Stan, Russell and many others put the "jig saw puzzle" back together again. But a concerted effort by MMM meant that the building was finished, the ribbon cut and the eager students were at their desks in a spacious classroom. Part of the MMM team also built a wide verandah onto the side of the main building.

1987

Finally the time had come to focus an MMM work party on finishing the kitchen and dining room. Two situations forced this move.

Matt Guidon, a young Swiss chef had arrived at Sherwood to cook in a cramped, primitive kitchen in the guard's room. That was a big adjustment from the modern Swiss restaurants in which he had trained.

Also, we were planning a big celebration in January 1988 for the 10th anniversary of Sherwood's ministry and the present conditions could not cater for the expected numbers.

Just before MMM arrived we had a visit from the area Health Commission. The inspector said that the guard's van kitchen did not meet the standards, as we were classified as a restaurant because seekers paid board. He looked uncertain when JP put his hand on his shoulder and said "Mate, you've come at the right time. Come and have a look at this!" JP led the inspector around between the two passenger carriages and into the unfinished new kitchen. "We have a building team arriving next week to finish off this kitchen, so tell me what all the restaurant rules are so we can comply with the standards."

Only three modifications were required and the MMM team happily did these, as well as working hard to enable us to move into our wonderful new kitchen and dining room. They also helped Russell to finish off the upstairs so that a lounge room, games area and pantry were completed.

1988

The new kitchen and dining room were put to the test at the 10-year celebrations in January. Hundreds of people joined us to praise God for His love and faithfulness. At 5.30pm the children's meals were served in two sittings in order to accommodate the 120 hungry little bodies. The rain eased by the time the adults were served with their meal, so they were able to fill the dining room and then spill out onto the verandah, patio, BBQ area and marquees to eat.

That year's MMM goal was to replace the men's goods-van bedrooms with better accommodation. Money and materials began arriving in answer to prayer so the old carriage was stripped bare and burned to the ground. A larger area was levelled, truckloads of gravel prepared the site, tranches were dug and foundation blocks laid.

One Wednesday morning JP laid out all the pipe fittings necessary to do the plumbing in the bathroom of this new bedroom block. Although not a plumber, he was armed with God's promise that *"I can do all things through Christ who strengthens me!"* (Philippians 4:13, NKJV)

At morning tea, a couple from WA drove in unannounced. They were *on the wallaby* (driving around Australia) and having heard about Sherwood they wanted to drop in for a few days to have a look. No-one ever just looks, so JP asked John and Elva what talents they had to share in exchange for their stay. JP gave a huge sigh of relief when John said that he was a plumber. By Thursday afternoon, John had the plumbing completed.

Through a generous donation, history was made! Previously all concrete had been mixed on site, but for the men's bedrooms three giant concrete trucks drove in and poured the ready-mixed concrete.

In June, the MMM team arrived under the leadership of Max Maddock once again. One of the team was a young German builder, Otto Rower, with whom a lifelong friendship and connection was forged. Max was concerned about the large number of concrete blocks to be laid in the allocated ten days. In answer to prayer, God prompted a local bricklayer and his labourer to help the team so the walls were up by the end of the first week. The roof and verandah were put on before the team left.

We thanked God for the practical work of MMM and for His listening, generous children who gave money for this job. The building was completely paid for and two of the bedrooms were already in use by the four men within the month.

The other two bedrooms and bathroom were soon completed. The building looked so good that it was suggested we rent out the motel-type rooms to staff for weekends off and call it *Cliff Views Holidays*.

1989

Just as there was a need to upgrade the seeker's accommodation, so there was a need to improve staff housing.

Plans were drawn up for a three-bedroom house with a separate one bedroom flat. Windows and doors from demolition jobs were restored and timber was allocated for the job. Three thousand dollars that was donated for building materials was used to purchase cypress flooring and red cedar for external cladding.

With MMM's annual visit the framework for the house was erected by expert builders. They worked long and hard so that by the end of two weeks, the house was at lock-up stage.

Glenn and the seekers worked on the house for the rest of the year. As Glenn was really a cabinetmaker, he said it was the biggest "cabinet" he had ever made. He transferred the same building principles to a much larger task.

MMM Work Team

1990

There were 23 in the MMM team that year as 15 students from the *Regents Park Christian Community School* added to the numbers.

The tasks they completed were, perhaps, not as striking in appearance as in previous years but they were greatly appreciated. Some were involved in concreting a large area of floor in the big shed – 72 square metres. This was achieved by mixing the concrete in small hand-driven mixers – there was not a ready-mix concrete truck in sight!

Others built a new chook shed (hen house) down the paddock, while others de-nailed timber and cleaned up blocks from the demolition of a restaurant at a local resort.

1991

For the first six months of the year Sherwood's numbers had grown, with forty-three people sitting down to meals in the dining room. This included ten seekers, their wives and seven of their children. The School now had eleven pupils. There were six pre-schoolers and one high schooler, Luke, who returned home on the weekends.

More accommodation was needed so preparations were made for the MMM team to construct a duplex for two families.

As the team worked from daylight to dark over the two weeks, our continual prayer was for safety, fellowship and accomplishment. By the time they left, the framework for the duplex was standing and the windows fitted. Part of the team constructed a mezzanine floor in the big shed to alleviate storage problems and to increase the usable workspace.

On the following two Saturdays, a group from Coffs Harbour tiled the duplex roof. Slowly and steadily staff and seekers completed the house. A very talented floor tiler just happened to be in the rehab program at the time and he tiled the bathrooms, toilets, laundries and kitchens in both units.

The first seeker family to occupy the new unit left their mark on our hearts – and on the walls, literally. Years of addiction had created a lot of pent up frustration in the family. One day the wife launched an attack on her lanky husband and swung a punch at his head. He ducked! She missed! But her fist punched a hole through the freshly plastered and painted wall. (Thankfully she didn't hit an underlying noggin of hard structural timber).

For quite a while the hole was covered with a painting hung strategically over the visible damage. But God had a beautiful plan to restore not just the hole in the wall, but to restore the relationship. When the husband came to the end of himself and called out to God for help, the healing began and the invisible pain was laid at the foot of Jesus' cross. The couple's relationship was revived, the children were lovingly restored and an amazing ministry resulted.

1992

God delights in *cliff-hangers*, that is, last minute miracles, because it ensures that we totally rely on Him as we have exhausted our own abilities. These miracles are so obviously His work that He receives the praise and we receive the blessing.

Whenever MMM are coming, the *cliff-hanger* miracles multiply and that year's construction of a mechanics' workshop was no exception. The foundations were laid and the rest of the structural materials were prayed for. The previous year JP had performed the wedding ceremony for a wealthy Coffs Harbour couple in Sydney. At the reception JP talked to a group of prominent businessmen. As the yacht gently bobbed at anchor in the Harbour one of the men promised to help at Sherwood if ever a need arose. Therefore JP wrote to him explaining what was needed to construct the workshop and asking for a quote for the best price that he could sell us these materials. The reply came back stating that the cost would be $200 to cover transport and the $3,000 worth of cladding would be free.

Structural timber and roofing were still required but they were promised from a local development proposal. At the last minute the Council refused permission for the development and we had only ten days to organise alternative materials before MMM's arrival. In answer to our urgent prayer we saw God organise the timber framing, the roofing iron and the arrival of the cladding in His perfect time. The new workshop cost a total of $2,000 in materials and the generous MMMers gave freely of their time. The workshop is 6x12 metres with two mechanical bays and a welding bay.

The sunnier location, particularly in winter is greatly appreciated. The old workshop was an adjunct to the generator shed so the quieter location is a more pleasant area in which to fix vehicles and to teach seekers the rudiments of mechanics.

1993

Usually an MMM work party is allocated to Sherwood just once a year because of their busy schedule, but that year was an exception.

In late January the old Butter Factory in Coffs Harbour was offered to us to demolish. This was at an inconvenient time to tackle such a large dangerous job outside the secure confines of Sherwood. New seekers need stability, minimal stress, and isolation from drugs during the early stage of their rehabilitation. The factory was in the middle of the city and had to be pulled down immediately. We needed outside help!

The old Coffs Butter Factory

God came to our aid, as He always does, by bringing along a group of MMMers, volunteers from the district and eight students from YWAM. (*Youth with a Mission*).

Safety was the main prayer request as the old building had suffered a lot of termite damage. As the men removed the iron from high up on the roof, they were standing on termite eaten beams. But, not a breath of wind blew to cause the building to sway.

The restoration of a nearby historic building (The Jetty Memorial Theatre) required red mahogany boards. The Theatre purchased $300 worth of boards from us, and it cost $290 for fuel for the Sherwood truck to transport the building materials home. The extra $10 was put towards hiring a jet ski in the Harbour as a special treat for all the hard workers.

God even provided drinks and ice creams for the workers on the job. In the back of the old factory a box with new windscreens was found and was sold to a local dealer for $100. The bill for the treats was $100.20 and the man at the shop was happy with $100 for the lot. The demolition was safely and successfully completed in two days, with the stockpile of building materials replenished at Sherwood.

The regular MMM team was due to arrive in May and their project was to link the big shed and the mechanic's workshop with a concrete floor and 16 metres of roofing. The MMMers started arriving on the Sunday and it was a great time of rejoicing as we met old friends and made new friends with those who had never been on a work party before. Roger Ward had been to Sherwood in January when the butter factory was demolished, but now he returned on his first official work party with his wife, Julie and little daughter Jessica. This was the beginning of a lifelong friendship and a future working relationship.

The story of God's provision of the money to pay for all the building materials was another *cliff-hanger* miracle, and is told in chapter ten.

During that visit the MMM team also built a little lounge and bathroom onto the side of Jack's caravan. What a blessing for a man who had blessed us so much over the years with his quiet, willing spirit and barrow loads of wood to keep the fires burning.

1994

During our family's sabbatical leave in Switzerland, a lovely MMM couple, Ray and June Dawson from the south coast, came to help out. Their wise counsel, life experiences and Godly enthusiasm encouraged staff and seekers alike.

A different perspective of a MMM work party was recorded by our cook, Ina. *"For me it was a new experience and a stretching time to be cooking for so many people – 66 in all. It was hectic but good. All the ladies from MMM were faithfully helping in the kitchen each day and I really enjoyed it. Also the little house I live in here at Sherwood has been extended".* Apart from adding two rooms onto Ina's house the MMM team tackled three other projects – and one was big and dangerous.

The school required a new roof and we initially considered using second hand materials. However, we felt prompted by God to order new material for the job at a cost of $1,200. The day after the roofing iron arrived, we received a cheque in the mail for $1,280 specifically designated for the school. The $80 expense for roofing screws was paid with the balance of the cheque.

The old roofing iron was removed and the new put on, all in one day. It's an extremely steep roof and we thanked God for not only the miraculous provision of the building materials, but also for safety as the men worked.

The Sherwood men had demolished a small demountable building previously and the MMM team re-erected it. There was still a lot of work to be done – plastering, electrical, plumbing and veranda – but the finishing off provided realistic job training and experience for the seekers.

This self-contained two-bedroom unit would then be used as emergency and visitor accommodation.

Also, some of the MMM team extended the workshop area to house the backhoe and fire tanker.

1995

Satan hates any signs of advancement in God's kingdom here on earth so the battle was raging. A quarterly praise letter was being compiled and an MMM team was due so the inevitable attacks were being manifested through people – seekers, staff, family and authorities. However, long ago we learned that we don't fight against "flesh and blood" so we don't focus on the person who delivers the blow – rather we fight in the spirit against "the powers of darkness." God's victories strengthen our faith.

The building of a storage shed *(YES ANOTHER SHED! All Australian boys need a shed...!!)* was planned and the $5,000 needed for its construction was in hand. However, Satan tried to use *the powers-that-be* to thwart *the Power-that-is!*

The local Council refused to pass our building plans, and even made the accusation that the previous Council had not passed the majority of buildings at Sherwood. We knew that this was an unfounded attack by Satan (*the father of lies*) as we had a filing cabinet full of plans that had been approved and stamped.

Addition of 3 extra classrooms to the School

Rather than cower, we chose to meet the attack head-on in God's strength. One of our Board Members was the Mayor of Coffs Harbour, so he and JP attended a meeting of our Shire Council (Pristine Waters) to present the truth. This show of strength and documentary evidence elicited an apology – stating that the recent Council amalgamation had confused their records. It also produced action!

Begrudgingly the Building Inspector checked the footings of the new shed and stamped our plans on the very day that MMM arrived to begin construction.

The large shed was completed in the two weeks – as well as many smaller and much appreciated jobs. The fellowship with these Godly folk was as important to us as the tasks that were completed.

1996

We were blessed with two MMM work parties in 1996 as Norm Foukes brought a team of Queensland Bible College students to Sherwood early in the year for a time of practical building experience. They added a feed storage area onto the dairy and insulated a flat. Their presence at devotions and their testimonies witnessed greatly to us all.

In early July we received a large donation specifically designated for school buildings. This unexpected money sent us to our knees to pray for wisdom. After prayer and consultation we drew up plans to add another three rooms to the existing schoolhouse – thus doubling the size of the building. The addition of a kitchen on the school's ablution block was also planned.

By October everything was in readiness for the MMM work party. Shire Council building permission had been received and the foundations were prepared. A small team of eight men and four ladies worked very hard over the next three weeks to bring the buildings to lock-up stage. Although the workload was enormous, the fellowship was sweet.

Dr Alan Roberts, a representative from the Sydney church that made the donation for the work, officially opened the Sherwood School extensions the following year. Also in attendance were the original two students who started their schooling here in 1983, Aaron Lockwood and Luke Reifler. Aaron was in his third year of Business management at the University in Coffs Harbour and Luke was in his second year of Primary Education at Lismore University. Other ex-students were in attendance and the current students presented items under the supervision of their teacher, Debbie Payne.

Luke & Aaron with the youngest student, Melody

1997

The best reason to demolish a church is because it has become too small for a growing congregation – as was the case of Sawtell Uniting. Thankfully MMM heard of this job and arranged for 11 of their people from NSW and Qld to assist us.

The work began on a Monday and the large A-frame building's cladding was removed by the next day. Wednesday it rained! At devotions that night there was a real spirit of thankfulness instead of the expected grumbling about the rain. B. praised God that the rain settled the dust so that his asthma was not aggravated. Because the carpet got wet, there were praise points for it now easily lifted off the timber floor.

By Thursday the job was successfully completed with truckloads of building material safely transported back to Sherwood. Five thousand bricks had been salvaged from the Church demolition and these were used to build curved walls on either side of the new front gates - a grand entrance into a little portion of God's work on earth – *Sherwood's Burly Gates*.

1998

Months before MMM's annual visit we prayerfully seek direction for the work projects that are to be tackled. That year three tasks were settled on: an extension to the office, the remodelling of a bathroom and the addition of two bedrooms onto a small house.

Apart from the physical work, which the MMMers achieve, they are also a blessing through their personal witness. Each night at devotions, a couple is given the opportunity to share their testimony of how they came to be serving God through this ministry. The majority of MMMers are retired folk. One worker quickly pulled Jen into line when she thanked God for the "oldies!" "We are recycled teenagers, thank you very much," he retorted. One young full-time worker shared how he saw an advertisement for tradesmen in his church bulletin and realised that he could be a tradesman and a missionary!

MMMers fulfil the words of an old Wesleyan Methodist Minister, Samuel Chadwick:

"Intensely spiritual, thoroughly practical & perfectly natural"

All Christians have the same employer – they just have different tasks.

1999

Another shed was constructed and it was like a mechanised "Amish barn raising". The upright posts were securely cemented into place and the modified roof trusses (from the

Sawtell church) neatly laid out in order. A beam welded onto the bucket of the backhoe lifted and positioned the trusses into place with some fine manoeuvring by the attached ropes. The trusses then had to be bolted onto the uprights – exactly matching the prepared holes.

Then it was time for the roof sheeting to go on – high above the ground at a steeply pitched angle. This potentially dangerous task was taken to God in prayer. Colin Nelson, a retired Anglican minister on team, awoke with the solution that had come to him in a dream. He told Ray Dawson and Roger Ward (the team leaders) the idea and soon a wooden *saddle* was constructed. This contraption was pulled up onto the apex of the roof and the men sat on it to screw down the sheeting. Thankfully the strong winds that were predicted by the weather bureau didn't eventuate before everything was screwed into place.

When the MMM ladies were not needed at the shed, they were busy helping with meals, gardening, mending and painting. Our prayers for safety, unity and productivity were certainly answered.

2000

God had already miraculously provided the money to build a 3-bedroom home so we eagerly welcomed the MMM team from NSW in early October.

Half the team concreted the floor of the bus shed that had been built the year before. The enormous floor area was covered with 20 cubic metres of concrete, which was mixed in a small electric mixer. The days were hot, the work was backbreaking and the men were mostly well into retirement age. Little by little they covered the vast space until one day the job was completed.

The other half of the MMM team built the house. Floor sections (from previous demolitions) were manoeuvred onto the stumps, frames erected, roof on, roofing screwed down, windows in and cladding nailed into place – a huge task for five older men in the space of three weeks.

Two weeks later a team from Qld spent a week putting plaster sheets up onto the internal walls and also building the veranda.

The MMMers were an inspiration to us all with their selfless, joyful service. The young seekers, who had often never known the fulfilment of work, were astounded - older seekers were challenged by the witness of changed lives - Staff were inspired, comforted and befriended - we were all blessed!

2001

Instead of concentrating on construction we were busy with weddings – three in fact. First Chantal & Colin Kemsley were married in July. Then in September Luke & Roslyna married, quickly followed by Shaun & Dearne Loone.

Finally it was time to get back onto the job and welcome a team of 15 eager MMMers in early November. A complex replacement of a pole in the main building, re-roofing of a house, and painting the bus shed were the major tasks completed in the ten days. Meanwhile, the women were busy and it was not until the January "spring clean" that their contribution was realised. The temperatures peaked at 45 degrees Celsius (108 F) that summer and we were very, very thankful that the MMM ladies had relieved us of the bulk of the work by washing windows, curtains and cupboards etc. in November, long before the excessive heat sapped our energy.

One young seeker commented, "These old blokes work hard, don't get paid and they can still smile. They must be on something!" They certainly were! They were *on* Jesus – grafted into Him, amazed by His grace and sustained by His presence.

2002

The annual 2-week MMM work party began and ended with a "snake". The first was only a look alike but was charged with 240 volts of electricity. Thankfully it did not discharge its "venom" when it was "decapitated" with a power saw.

The second was a real one, whose presence wasn't appreciated when it joined some of the men on a final inspection of the building site.

It was good to have Roger Ward leading the team again and looking so well after his kidney transplant earlier in the year. The 2002 project was the re-modelling of the "chalet". This building began with two railway goods wagons placed in the open paddock 25 years before. By roofing over the wagons and blocking in the ends of the space between, a special home had been created for staff and seekers. However the time had come to replace, restore and remodel the tired building to enable it to serve for many more years to come.

2003

Two properties, five kilometres down the road from Sherwood Cliffs ,were purchased through a murder, suicide and miraculous baby. The only house on one property was unfinished and there were no buildings on the second one. But the MMM team couldn't stroll along the jetty, or loll around the beaches or smile like the Big Banana – there was work to be done!

They concentrated on finishing off the house at Sherwood Tobiah. Internal walls were lined, the verandahs completed, gutters installed, an art studio constructed and a shed was turned into a future office. Some of the team put the finishing touches on the chalet which they had worked on the previous year.

While the men built, the women painted, cleaned, gardened and blessed us with their wise counsel. God has a big family and it's always nice to spend time with the relatives.

2004

The Wards had been State leaders of MMM so, when they came onto Sherwood staff, we now had a daily connection with this wonderful ministry. Julie wrote in the Praise Letter, *"Having come to Sherwood on MMM work teams over the past 11 years we saw a different side being on the receiving end. It was such a blessing and encouragement…Roger was kept busy running between the two roles of keeping the team with enough work and materials plus fulfilling his responsibilities on staff…"*

A pre-fabricated shed had been ordered and scheduled for delivery well before the team was due to arrive. A concrete slab had been poured and block work completed. But, alas, the shed did not arrive!

What do you do when you have an eager team of 12 tradesmen all ready and rearing to go…and not a steel stud or noggin in sight? You rearrange the work of course! Jobs that had been put on the *back burner* were now achievable. A roof was built over a shipping container, a spiral staircase installed in the chalet, a concrete slab poured in the caravan park, repairs made to the dairy, handrails installed and electrical work completed.

We have learned that *GOD'S TIMING IS AS IMPORTANT AS GOD'S LEADING* so we rejoiced in all that was achieved.

2005

We welcomed that year's team with open arms; sharing our home, hearts and *belly bug*. Within a day of their arrival they were dropping with a horrible gastro-intestinal malady that had been plaguing the north coast since Easter. Their usual buoyant natures would be a little subdued over lunch, stoically upright at afternoon tea, but by the evening they would have succumbed and crawled off into bed. Twenty fours later they would be back at work – a little wobbly at the knees and pale in the face – but determinedly, back at work.

When the land was being cleared at Sherwood Glen, all the millable trees were set aside – tallow wood, bloodwood, flooded gum and red mahogany. A saw miller had offered to cut up these trees with his portable sawmill, but, he was only available during the three weeks that MMM was with us. That was perfect timing as two men were allocated to the tailoring-out position while the Sherwood men stacked and bundled the timber for drying and transported the off-cuts home for firewood. A 3-car garage was constructed with this timber – giving rise to a comment that "there were still leaves on it".

Lots of other building jobs were completed, as well as plumbing, guttering and electrical.

Completion of first building at Sherwood Glen

The women were just as busy, and sometimes just as dirty, as the men. They completely painted out a staff house, and a carport plus gardening, mending and sewing curtains.

2006

Caravans, campers and motorhomes filled the grounds and the dining room was bursting at the seams with 25 energetic and enthusiastic MMMers.

The major task for the year was to erect a shed at Sherwood Glen. Recent heavy rains had made the track impassable for heavy concrete trucks. Although the shed site had been prepared it was impossible to pour the concrete and therefore its construction could not begin. Even the building materials couldn't be delivered to the site with the soggy roads. So tonnes of tiles and truckloads of gravel filled the wettest holes. Culverts and pipes drained the water off the road.

Rather than have the MMMers relax in the "resort" (the *last resort* for many) Roger organised all the men to demolish a church hall in Woolgoolga. The original plan was for half the team to do the demolition, while the other half constructed the shed. Now, everyone was involved in gathering this valuable building material.

Finally, the road dried up enough for the trucks to get through and eight metres of concrete were poured. The team then set to work on the adult-size meccano construction. By the end of the third week the shed was up – the first building for the women's rehabilitation centre.

2007

We had hoped that the MMMers would be able to make a start on constructing the houses at Sherwood Glen, but Council's delay in approving the Development Application showed that God had other plans for the team.

Georgie's little house had a larger bathroom added and the Ward's pergola was replaced. The most taxing task was to strengthen and straighten the poles on the verandah of the main building. Over the years some of the poles had sunk a bit deeper into the ground and some had deteriorated with rot. John, the electrician, diligently and quietly worked his way through repairing washing machines and attending to lighting problems.

During that time two ex-seekers, Rusty and David, visited and they shared about their Christian journeys, which included time spent at Sherwood - an encouragement to us all.

On the last day of the MMMers visit we received the long-awaited (three years!) word from the Council that approval had been finally given to commence building at Sherwood Glen. Seven cabins, three staff homes and one multi-purpose building could be built. Even though JP couldn't convince the team to extend their time, they assured us that, God willing, they would be back!

2008

It was a very busy start to the year with celebrating Sherwood's 30 years of ministry to those caught in the drug scene. When Julie and Roger went off on a well-deserved sabbatical trip around Australia, God brought their friends from Victoria to help out.

Allen and Bronwyn Ronalds had worked with MMM on many projects and now Allen supervised Sherwood Glen's construction for three months. During this time God sent along plasterers, roof plumbers, carpenters, bricklayers, electricians and labourers.

Allen & Bronwyn Ronalds

During the MMM visit a terrible accident occurred. Ruth Nelson fell from her caravan step and broke her hip and wrist. While waiting for the ambulance, we made Ruth as comfortable as possible until her husband, Colin, who had been working at the Glen, joined her. Apart from worrying about leeches as she lay on the damp ground, she was also concerned that her accident would interfere with a wedding ceremony scheduled for that afternoon. While Josh and Hannah were saying their vows, Ruth was transported to Coffs Hospital for surgery. She was delighted to know that she hadn't interrupted the wedding and we were delighted to know that this plucky, brave woman was healing well.

2009

For the first three weeks in March, Sherwood was buzzing with excitement as the MMM team was here. They focused on building cabins at the Glen. At the end of a very busy first day, the floors and wall frames were up on cabin number five.

The tongue and groove flooring, purchased from a local mill, was laid in the staff houses while verandahs were being built on other cabins.

The shed that MMM had previously built made an ideal under-cover workspace. Trestles were set up in there and countless strips of timber were painted before being attached to the appropriate buildings.

There was an urgency to pray for MMM as its major base in Whittlesea, Victoria, had been destroyed by bushfire. The new NSW base at Wyee was under construction and required a lot of wisdom, finance and trade skills. We prayed for these needs as well as for new members to swell the ranks of this valuable ministry whose motto is, *"SERVING THOSE WHO SERVE"*.

2010

Trevor and Janette Watts led the team and their final praise point at MMM's last devotions with us was: "Praise God for a great team. Two months ago we only had two couples. Look at all that has been achieved with 11 willing tradesmen and workers".

The Glen once again received the most attention with painting, interior electrical lighting, plumbing and installation of kitchen cupboards. Because of the distance from mains power, solar panels would produce all the electricity. The $180,000 we were quoted to bring mains power into the valley was used, instead, to set up a total solar system with a diesel generator as a back up for prolonged overcast weather. The MMM team poured concrete pads for the solar batteries on each of the main buildings. No sooner had the cement blocks gone up for the soundproof generator shed, than it was being painted.

Gwen created beautiful curtains from old ones from a local resort and her husband, Bill, hung them professionally on all the windows.

Sherwood Cliffs received some attention with a new external staircase, rendering of brick walls and replacing the school fence. Those willing workers achieved a great deal during their stay.

2011

The Glen was open and operating as a women's rehab under the management of Colin and Chantal Kemsley.

A three bay carport was the main project for MMM that year. Because Kemsley's house was the only place for communal activities, we seized the opportunity to give them some privacy by adding a studio, counselling room and storerooms to the carport – away from their house. Most of the MMMers were well into their 70's and praying for strength to stand the frames for the additions. God answered by sending two builders from Coffs, Alex and Ken, who just happened to be between jobs. Their younger age and agility were greatly appreciated. Modifying huge steel beams from a previous demolition created the framework for the carport. The loader raised up the beams and held them in place so they could be braced together.

Colin & Ruth Nelson, Ruth & Bruce Walker

While the men worked at the Glen, Janette diligently painted her way through a 4-bedroom staff house at Sherwood Cliffs. A little extra water in the paint ensured that the pain ran out when the last wall was done.

We never thought that we would ever have Colin and Ruth Nelson plus Bruce and Ruth Walker on a MMM job at Sherwood again because of major health issues. But here they were – both couples, together at the same time even though Ruth Nelson required a walking stick from her fall in 2008. With their Godly natures and cheeky sense of humour we were greatly blessed with their presence.

2012

In early June four couples and two single men came to Sherwood for R & R. As Bill said, "This did not mean a Rest and Recreation but rather Repair and Renovation".

The chook shed and carport at the Glen were finished off with gutters, locks, bracing and glass. Verandah rails were tediously fitted at Tobiah. Houses were renovated at Sherwood Cliffs for new staff and the annual reorganisation of the linen room was completed.

2013

For the first time in 30 years we weren't blessed with a MMM team as they were required in more places than they had people willing and available to meet all the needs.

2014

Caravans and campers once again filled the school grounds, houses were occupied and there was a sense of excitement with that years' team of MMMers.

Their two weeks flew by with the large task of re-oiling all the western red cedar cladding on six houses. Other jobs included modifications to a shipping container, overhauling the plumbing, electrical re-wiring, replacing a verandah, re-erecting a tank stand and building a staircase. When the important sewing of curtains was completed I imposed on the willing workers to make me lots of warm pouches for young wildlife in my care.

Peter Groves celebrated his 70th birthday at Sherwood and he shared his testimony of how he became a Christian. He acknowledged how God had brought him from England to meet his future wife, Lyn, in New Zealand. Together they had enjoyed God's presence and guidance over many years and He was still with them right up to that day.

2015

That year's small team solved many problems with big results. Gwen commandeered Marion's house and sewing machine and produced beautiful curtains, pot mitts and storage bags. Sally and Ellen were quickly absorbed into the kitchen helping with the *Timber Fest* preparations and processing the abundance of vegetables from the garden. Lots of fellowship was enjoyed over a potato peeler and a sewing needle!

The MMM men fixed leaking taps, re-wired screen doors and sorted out electrical problems. But the biggest job was solving the termite and dry rot damage in Kemsley's house. Stealthily those hungry little critters had chewed their way through a lot of the structural timber – all the way to the roofline. Weakened boards were replaced but the attempted destruction of the termites is a continuing problem.

2016

Another small team of MMMers who took on a small, but very important project: the remodelling of a bathroom. This required the old tiles, tub, shower and toilet to be removed before the work could begin. The dark brown bathroom was changed into a lighter and more functional area.

After her husband Bruce's death, Ruth Walker drove her camper van here from the central coast. She declared war on weeds as she worked her way around all the gardens.

2017

Sadly, no MMM party was available again that year.

Without MMM's regular visits our living conditions would be far more primitive. We thank God for raising up such an organisation to bless so many – us included. May God bless them all richly, abundantly and beyond measure in return.

Chapter Nine

PERSONAL ATTACKS

1973

Our first year in Perth was spent living in a downtrodden inner city suburb. JP worked amongst youth with an Aboriginal Church while I started my Occupational Therapy studies. We rented half way between a nightclub and a wine saloon, with an infamous park around the corner (commonly called *Metho Park*). We were strategically placed for a steep learning curve!

JP felt led to organise a Saturday night outreach in the park where drinkers gathered in the dark recesses.

During the week before the first outreach I was continually given the same verse from the Bible – *"...do not fear those who kill the body but cannot kill the soul. But rather fear Him who is able to destroy both soul and body in hell."* (Matthew 10:28 - NKJV). Although I was scared, I honestly told God that I didn't think that I could trust Him completely to keep us safe. However, I was willing to give it a go.

Lewis strummed his guitar while Margaret and I sang an old favourite mission hymn. Our feeble voices were interrupted by screaming from two frightened young women on the other side of the park. A hulking, big man who was obviously very drunk was chasing them. When he saw the girls hide behind us he smashed his beer bottle against a tree and lumbered menacingly toward us.

JP stepped up to the microphone and calmly said, "G'day folks. My name's John and we're here to tell you that God loves you." He then launched into singing "The Old Rugged Cross" while the drunk man stumbled onwards with the broken beer bottle in hand and colourful curses spewing out of his mouth.

This is what you warned me about all week, Lord, I fearfully prayed. *You will have to take control of this situation. Please help us!*

About a metre before us, the man stopped, dropped to his knees and let the broken bottle slip from his hand. Curses turned to heart-wrenching sobs as we continued singing. Finally he quietened down, stood up and asked if he could sing with us. By the time the Outreach was finished all eyes were on us: *Was our Christianity only words? Would we leave an obviously distressed man behind in the park?* We learned that he had been released from prison in the morning, had swapped his return ticket home to Kalgoorlie for *grog* and he had nowhere to sleep.

We just knew that we couldn't leave him there so I prayed for continuing safety and we took him home. After settling him in a spare bedroom I wanted to lock our bedroom door. "If we're going to trust God to look after us we shouldn't do that," JP said. He quickly fell asleep but I was still wide-awake when I heard footsteps in the hallway.

"Wake up!" I hissed as I shoved JP out of bed. When he returned he said that the man wanted to go, so he had wandered off into the darkness.

This incident increased our faith in trusting God for protection. It also made us aware that we needed to be willing to <u>not only talk</u> about God's love...but also to <u>show it</u>.

1978

Sin stains the soul. This was very evident when a pretty, blonde 22-year old came to Sherwood for help. Naively,

Tracey (not her real name) had been lured to Sydney with the offer of a glamorous photographic modelling job only to find that it was a front for prostitution. Her withdrawal from the mind numbing drugs that enabled her to be a prostitute was silently endured, but her need to shower five times a day was her way of trying to cleanse her body.

One day a car had stopped at the front gate and two men, with binoculars, were scanning the property. JP's demand to know what they were up to elicited this response. "We're looking for one of our girls and we heard that she is here. There's a big convention in Coffs this weekend and we need extra working girls." With an indifferent shrug of his shoulders he continued, "I'm sure she could use the money and we'll return her to you on Monday.""No way!" JP hotly replied. "She's finished with that lifestyle. Get off my property or you'll be sorry!"

The next day, Max and JP were down the paddock planting cucumbers when they noticed a car stopped out on the main road. As they stared at the familiar two men, Max yelled "Duck!" Bullets zinged through the air just as Max and JP fell to the ground. The car hurriedly drove off while dirt was wiped away from two ashen faces. "Thanks Lord" they stammered. "Thanks for saving us."

Tracey was relieved to be protected and began to enjoy a drug free life. The number of showers decreased as the blood of Christ washed the stains on her soul.

1980

Although we live with people who have often had a long criminal history and violent behaviour we have been protected. An unexpected attack came, not from a Seeker, but from a visitor's father.

On our first Sunday back in Coffs Harbour, a woman demanded to know what had happened during our recent trip to Switzerland. She said that she had been woken up and urged to pray for our safety on a certain night at a certain time. "I felt that you were in great danger," she said.

JP realised that her feeling of urgency was exactly when his life was being threatened.

A young man who had found Jesus during a visit to Sherwood, had encouraged JP to visit his family. Polite greetings were exchanged and then JP was taken into an upstairs office. The young man's father closed and locked the door behind them before producing a gun. With a shaking hand he pointed the weapon at JP's head. Furiously he said, "I'm going to kill you! You've ruined my life! Because of you my child has become a religious fanatic and my plans for his future are destroyed." JP silently called out to God for help as he assessed the distance to the window and how he could jump through it. The man's finger tightened on the trigger while his face flushed with emotion. Time stood still - slowly he lowered the gun and said in a barely controlled voice, "Get out!"

Chapter Ten

AUDACIOUSNESS

A dear friend, an ex-work colleague, encouraged me to write a chapter on JP's audaciousness – his boldness. Ruth Walker said, *"JP's directive to 'GET UP YOU STUPID WOMAN'* in this politically correct age of coaxing and cajoling is so typical of him. His frankness cuts to the quick, but after the initial shock, inspires confidence in so many.

"There would be times when it's got him into trouble, but if there's one aspect of JP's character that God has gifted him with (outside of the spiritual) is this bold, exasperating frankness."

1980

When JP was off the property one day a very troubled seeker started 'fitting'. She thrashed about on my lounge room floor, jerking violently, eyes rolled back and mumbling incoherently. Joanne and I took it in turns to comfort her while the other one ensured the stability of the rest of the community. We talked gently to her, mopped her brow, cradled her head and prayed fervently.

When we were both nearing exhaustion, JP finally returned to hear of our dilemma. He took one look at the prostrate figure, pushed her with his foot and firmly said ,"Get up you stupid woman!" Obediently she did!

Joanne and I were so stunned with her immediate response that we didn't have the energy to thank him...or to 'kill' him for leaving us to struggle through. She made slow progress that year, but returned a few years later to continue her rehabilitation.

1978

Large, pine packing cases, donated from a manufacturing factory, were a perfect way to line the breezy, louvered carriages – except they were incredibly rough and splintery. A machine to plane the surface was needed and so, prayed for.

While shopping on Friday, JP noticed the exact planer, on special, in a hardware store. "Put it aside please," he asked. "I'll be back on Monday to pay and pick it up." By faith, he thanked God that He would provide, and continued with his shopping.

On returning to Sherwood, he learned that two ladies had visited and they both left envelopes containing money. The combined donations exactly matched the cost of the planer.

1979

A ride-on mower was needed to keep the fast-growing grass down. After praying, JP felt he should spend two hundred dollars, and no more.

When he saw the exact mower needed, but unpriced, he asked the seller, "How much do you want for it?"

"You can have it for $200," the seller replied. JP accepted the price and organised to pick it up and pay the following day – even though he didn't have the money.

However, our wonderful Lord who promises to meet all of our needs prompted one of His obedient children to give the $200. The giver did not know of our need, but by faith and obedience, he posted a donation for Sherwood the week before the mower was seen.

The money arrived the day of the transaction.

1982

The Bible says *FEED MY SHEEP*, not to *FLEECE MY SHEEP*. 'Feeding' results in blessing – 'Fleecing' (swindling) results in dishonour and disgrace.

A... became a Christian, but the years of drug taking had scarred his mind. During a delusional phase he wanted to withdraw his life savings from the bank, stand on a headland and let all of the money blow away in the breeze.

"This world's systems are evil," A... ranted. "I don't want to be part of it!"

Calmly JP suggested that he use the money for good, rather than waste it.

"I'll give it to Sherwood then," A... retorted "No, use it for something else," JP said.

"If you won't take it for Sherwood then I'll throw it off the headland." "Okay", JP finally agreed. "You fill out the withdrawal slip and I'll fix it up in town today."

The Bank Manager listened to JP's story and suggestion and agreed to set up a trust fund for A... When A...'s mother was contacted, she was relieved to hear of that solution, as she feared he would be swindled out of the $10,000, or rashly lose it.

Years later, when A...'s mind had cleared he excitedly telephoned about his plans to go to Bible college in Tasmania. "Please pray that I will be able to save the money needed," he asked.

"Your need has already been met," JP smugly replied. "God has already provided!"

A... was amazed to hear of the trust fund and the management of his money during his unstable time of life.

Even today, A…'s mental health is still precarious (compounded by the death of his wife) but the presence of Jesus comforts him.

1993

As the time drew closer for MMM's annual visit, advice was sought on steel construction, plans were drawn and submitted to Council, the site was levelled and cost estimates were made. However there was no money for the job! At times doubts assailed us! The more we took the need to God, the more we felt that we were to proceed and trust Him to supply. Finally, putting doubts aside and stepping out by faith, JP ordered all the materials, the week before MMM was due to start work.

Trucks arrived with gravel, eight tonne of cement bags piled up, sheets of iron and fibreglass stacked up and steel beams were trucked in from Sydney. But still no money! Although our faith was small, we had faith in a big God!

The work commenced with great gusto early Monday morning and we continued to thank God that He would supply. When the mail was opened on Wednesday night there was a moment of incredulous silence. Noisy rejoicing soon followed as two envelopes containing cheques for $7,800 were waved aloft. Jehovah Jireh! Truly, God is our provider.

That night at devotions, as we all sat around the meal tables, we gave thanks to God for His miraculous provision and for His listening saints who heard His prompting and responded so generously. That money covered the costs of all the materials for the workshop training area.

2007

A worried parent talked to JP about his daughter's escalating problems from her abuse of drugs.

"Why is it that most of the rehabs are Christian based, and if not, they don't seem to work?" the concerned parent asked.

JP's earthy, logical response was, "If you find a fault in something you buy, you take your warranty claim back to the manufacturer. It's the same with people who have a spiritual problem. God exists! God made mankind! By taking the warranty claim to Him, you get fixed up. This is called FAITH and it works, because it's God's work!"

JP continued, "When I walk down the Mall and see all the drop-outs and drug addicts, I get excited because I can see the potential they have, if they come to Christ. My hope is not in what they could do, or in my ability to help them, but my hope is in Christ. He's their Manufacturer and He's waiting for them to present their warranty claim!"

Chapter Eleven

ACCIDENTS HAPPEN

Stan's free ride!

2004

A praise point one evening from a seeker, was ,"I think you could get shot at Sherwood and wouldn't get hurt!"

Abandonment to God is not reckless, irresponsible living, but recognition that as His blood-bought children, we can "approach the throne of grace with confidence, so that we may receive mercy and find grace to help us in our time of need" (Hebrews 4:16).

That day the seeker had witnessed two obvious miracles attesting to God's protection. The men had winched a 100kg roller door into place in the new shed at Tobiah. Roger was standing beneath two trestle ladders when the knot in the supporting rope gave way and the heavy roller door crashed down. Roger's glasses were knocked off his face but the door politely landed on the ladders, only one metre below – instead of ending up on the concrete floor, three metres below. A gasp of thankful praise arose from the men, in particular from Roger. Neither the door nor the glasses were damaged.

On that same day the heavy-duty scaffolding was being removed from the Reifler's lounge room as all the cracks in the cathedral ceilings had been sealed. JP was up on the scaffolding when he removed a brace, causing it to scissor apart. The other men were at the opposite end of the room, but Thomas was working close by. Instantaneously he jumped up and caught the falling piece before it hit the floor. Neither Thomas nor JP were hurt – and the floor wasn't damaged.

A few days earlier, the seeker was once again in the right place at the right time to witness God's protective power at work. He and Paul had just returned 35 senior citizens to Coffs Harbour in the coach after they had enjoyed an outing to Sherwood.

While refuelling at the service station Paul noticed a 30mm split along the beading of one tyre. The seeker who had worked as a tyre fitter advised caution. When the offending tyre was removed it was noticed that the other inside front tyre had split, almost the whole way around. This was only obvious because the first tyre had been removed for repair.

Apologetically, Paul presented us with a $1,000 bill for two new tyres when he returned home. We rejoiced with their awareness of the problems, the safety for all using the coach and that God had already provided for one tyre through the generous donation of the visiting group (who gave before the need was evident).

1979

"I wonder if mum has cooked my favourite chicken and asparagus dish?" I thought as we headed west to visit my parents for the weekend.

JP and Leo chatted away in Swiss German while Sylvia and I entertained young Luke in the back seat of our Valiant station wagon. It was getting darker when we drove over a blind crest and toward a one-lane bridge at the bottom of a steep hill. A *ute* (utility) was approaching from the other side, but as he had the 'Give Way' sign we didn't slow down.

To our horror he kept on coming! There was no way to avoid crossing the bridge as the banks of the river dropped away steeply on either side. "Hold on!" JP yelled. "This is it Lord. Here we come," I whispered.

The two cars reached the centre of the bridge at the same moment. Time stood still! We looked directly into the face of a bleary eyed, unshaven man with a terrified expression.

Door handles scraped together with a sickening screech. But miraculously the two cars passed each other on that narrow, one-lane bridge. With unbelievable relief we shouted out our praises to God and *thawed out* from our frozen state of fear.

Although that bridge has now been superseded I always look at it and marvel at our protection on that dark night. It wasn't our time to meet our Maker personally.

1994

Excitement was bubbling up as we, the Reifler family, had just left Sherwood for our trip to Switzerland. Mike Vos was driving us to the airport and we were fast approaching the crossroads at Nana Glen.

A brand new, one hundred thousand dollar school bus had halted at the stop sign then proceeded across the intersection.

The driver had not seen us approaching on her right on the main road as we must have been in the shadow of the trees when she looked. Halfway through the intersection she was horrified to see our car hurtling toward her. Immediately she slammed her foot on the brakes and the bus slowed, but strangely would not stop. The car was still coming! Desperately she then tried to accelerate out of the way.

"Your car was level with the front door of my bus," the driver said, "and I waited for the impact, but nothing happened! I looked around and saw that your car was miraculously on the other side of my bus and continuing on its way to Coffs Harbour."

The whole hair raising event was over in the blink of an eye. We were so caught up in the frenzy of the trip that we did not realise the enormity of God's protection until the bus driver, a dear friend Gayl Ellem wrote to us in Switzerland.

1979

Bob, a friend from Church was struggling to give up smoking and one evening, on the spur of the moment, he decided to drive out to Sherwood and talk to JP. He drove via the isolated State Forestry roads but half way into the trip skidded on the rough gravel surface. As he careered down a steep slope he lost control of the car and crashed into a muddy bank. "I looked death in the eye," Bob said when his car came to a shuddering halt. The mudguard was pushed into the tyre and the car was stuck in a ditch.

Through gritted teeth Bob dejectedly said ,"Thank you Lord." It was a dark, moonless night, he had no torch, his wife didn't know where he was, we didn't know he was on his way out, he had no phone, no reference points and there was no passing traffic on this isolated bush track.

"My only hope is to get help from JP," Bob thought. With slippers on his feet, and carrying a package of frozen fish he set off on what he supposed was a 5-6km walk. The night was so dark that Bob could only keep to the main track by shuffling his feet along the grass edges. When a kangaroo hopped close by Bob said, "It scared six months growth out of me!" Owls swished past his face and strange noises emanated from the surrounding bush. Were dingoes tracking him? Bob comforted himself with the thought the animals wouldn't hurt him. "My only hurt will come from getting lost," he muttered to himself.

After two hours, alone and in the dark Bob had walked 12 kilometres. The "Sherwood" lights guided him in. For some unknown reason the generator had not been switched off at 10pm (unusual for this *regular-as-clockwork* Swiss). As the thumping of the generator faded away, we heard a blood-curdling scream for help from the paddock. After a consoling cup of tea near the warm fire we managed to prise the frozen fish out of Bob's equally frozen fingers.

Once Bob was "thawed" he and JP headed off in the Land Cruiser with a crow bar and chains. The mudguard was soon straightened out, the car pulled back onto the road and Bob was able to be back home by midnight.

Six months later Bob was so challenged by smoking that he threw his cigarettes away. His wise words were, "You're only skidding your wheels if you are not genuine. Without conviction you can't get free."

2005

The switch that signalled when the bore was pumping wasn't working, so Paul set out to fix it. The water tank is situated on a ledge about 20 metres up the cliff face. A fallen branch had immobilized the indicator switch on the side of the tank.

Paul set up an aluminium folding ladder and climbed up to check the switch. Suddenly the ladder's safety clips gave way! Paul's left hand clutched the side of the tank while his left leg was tangled in the collapsed ladder. If he fell he would probably break bones, roll down the cliff and not be missed for hours. He said, "Panic wasn't an option," so he prayed, "Lord, I could really use some help here."

With a clear head, he lifted the ladder up with his free right leg until his right hand could hold it. He then extricated his trapped leg, positioned the ladder against the tank and pushed himself up onto the top of the tank. Then he could pull the ladder up with him and was able to clip the legs firmly in place. Finally it was safe to climb back down. Paul said that he could sense a calm logic take over after he prayed. "God is there in the crowd, as well as when you are on your own," he testified.

Honi's tumble into the dairy "poo" cart!

Chapter Twelve

MECHANICAL MIRACLES

1976

The South Australian Christian Endeavourers hired our 18-year-old Bedford bus to take them on a Pilbara Pilgrimage of gospel music shows. When we picked them up in Perth they were a bit dismayed at the age of our vehicle.

The convoy set off north with a Toyota minibus carrying nine passengers plus musical instruments and some stage sets: A Valiant station wagon with four passengers and towing a 4-wheel trailer carrying a huge box full of stage equipment, and our old Bedford bus with 34 passengers and lots of personal luggage.

First stop was Geraldton where JP acquired a large roof rack, which he removed from a disused Mission bus. Now that the luggage was on the roof, the passengers had much more legroom to face the hundreds of kilometres ahead.

About 30kms before Tom Price the Valiant skidded on the newly graded dirt road, causing the trailer to roll over. The ½ inch (1¼ cm) metal tongue of the tow bar twisted 90 degrees, allowing the trailer to roll over, without taking the car with it. No one was injured but extensive damage was sustained to the contents of the box, including expensive stage equipment. After a wheel was replaced the trailer was towed into town and an "army" of locals and Endeavourers repaired the damage so that the show could go on.

On the way into Wittenoom, a stone thrown up from an overtaking vehicle smashed the passenger side windscreen of the bus. Although the hot travellers appreciated the extra fresh air, the smothering red dust was not! A direct quote from a report, North West Endeavour '76 by Barry Fopp continues the story:

"Bedford windscreens are not the easiest things to come by anywhere these days and the chances of getting one out in the heart of the Pilbara would seem, at best, quite remote. However, by this time, we had learnt that the seemingly impossible was quite the norm to John. We were not surprised the following morning to learn that he had visited a property some miles out of Wittenoom where, he had heard, there was a bus lying idle because its driver side windscreen had been smashed. How could we not just stand in awe at the way the Lord was providing for our every need?

"With another day and a half to go on dirt roads though, John decided to postpone fitting the new windscreen. With more than adequate fresh air inside the bus we left Wittenoom to travel to Newman."

1977

From an orange Kombi bus in 1972 when we headed to Western Australia, we were now returning to the eastern states in a convoy of vehicles that my father dubbed *"THE SOUL BROTHERS CIRCUS."*

With our 4-month-old baby, Luke, we were in the Bedford bus, my brother and sister-in-law drove the Toyota van, Stuart and Liz Walker and Max Lambadgee drove their Land Cruiser with caravan attached, and Daniel Bosshard was in the station wagon.

The Nullabor was behind us when, 30kms west of a small desert town, Wilcannia, Stuart's water pump blew up and his radiator blocked in the 44-degree heat. Gazing at the escaping steam JP remarked, "It's just as well that the bus had its service. I'll tow you in!" The extraordinary sight of a Land Cruiser and caravan being towed by an old Bedford bus created a great deal of curiosity in Wilcannia.

"Where are you going?" spectators asked. "Over to Coffs Harbour to set up a drug rehabilitation farm" JP replied.

"Who cares about drug addicts", one bystander sniffed. "They're just getting what they deserve." "Well, God cares about them and so do we" JP replied. "And God cares about you as well!"

Finding spare parts for Stuart's Land Cruiser in this isolated, boarded up, far western town could have been a problem – if God wasn't on the job. The one and only garage had nothing! When JP asked at the General Store if they might have a water pump for a FJ45 Land Cruiser we were amazed at the response. The shopkeeper reached up to a top shelf, blew the dust off a box and said, "Three years ago we ordered this water pump for a Telecom vehicle. They never picked it up. So, I guess it's yours!" The water pump kit was quickly installed, as it was a perfect fit – from our perfect God.

2005

A Coffs Harbour businessman gave Sherwood a dual cab Nissan Navara Ute that would be good for carrying guys and gear between the three properties. It needed a new gearbox, but Paul was so inundated with mechanical repairs that the ute sat in the shed, untouched, for three months. Finally, he was able to give JP a detailed description of a replacement gearbox that would be needed. JP rang the wrecker who said, "You could be lucky! That particular model is hard to find spare parts for, but I just bought one this morning from Sydney. I only need the motor. I guess the gear box is yours!"

God's timing is always perfect.

2009

Many Aussies find it hard to speak openly about God and they use vague euphemisms to indicate their awareness of His existence. Because we believe in miracles (and totally depend on them) many "non-churchy" people tell us of their encounters with the Divine. Hesitantly, they call it a coincidence, but really, they want us to recognise the evidence of a loving God at work for them.

Our old (40 years+) Massey Ferguson tractor was having its gear box overhauled when JP discovered that he needed a special hardened steel pin. The spare part dealer said that neither he, nor anybody else, would have such a specialised pin – one with a hole in the middle to fit into a 4mm space. Without this pin, the hydraulics on the tractor wouldn't work. The dealer walked back into his workshop to get something else and then quickly returned. "Look what I just happened

Mechanical Miracles

to spot on the workshop floor!" he said to JP, holding up the exact pin required.

Laconically, the dealer continued, "Why do you worry! He (*pointing upwards*) seems to look after you."

The old tractor, 1978

Chapter Thirteen

ANGELS – AWARES AND UNAWARES

1976

As preparation for the future work, we were grown through many experiences in Perth. One was through a glimpse into God's protection by His angelic beings.

Every Friday night we drove our old bus to a housing commission suburb to collect young people for a fun youth group gathering. Most of the teenagers met us in a carpark shared by a shopping centre, hotel and TAB. When the bus pulled in an eager group of Nyoongar (the local indigenous tribe) kids greeted us. However a belligerent cohort of *Wadjelas* (white fellas) hurled abuse at us. They were asked to join in but always rudely refused.

One evening, youth group was over, most of the teenagers delivered safely back to their homes, when JP decided that he needed to visit a distraught family. He parked the bus behind a block of housing commission units and across from the hotel car park.

After a busy week at University I was tired and eager to head home. My two companions, Victor and Cissy were equally ready for bed, as their school studies in the city, far from their Kimberley families, were exhausting. Wearily we sat and chatted while an old man in the back of the bus snored loudly and was cared for by his little grandson. They were hitching a ride back to the suburb where we lived.

With a timid voice the little boy shook his grandfather and said that he could see a big crowd of rough-looking youths ominously gathered under the street light near the hotel. We too saw them and realised that they were pointing at our bus, parked in the dark, lonely carpark of the units. Quickly, I tried to lock the bus door but it was impossible from the inside. There was nothing to barricade it shut and so we were in a very vulnerable situation.

The teenagers were arming themselves with sticks and rocks as they advanced menacingly toward us. All we could do was pray. Victor, Cissy and I knelt down on the floor of the bus. "Lord, we ask that you would protect us," we urgently prayed. "Send your angels to guard us!"

As we tried to pray with confidence, the little boy in the back gave a frightened commentary of the mob's movements and the old man woke from his drunken stupor. He moaned loudly and fearfully while the boy's insistent screams of terror mingled with our less than confident prayers. The violent language from the mob grew louder as they drew close to our exposed position. Their description of what they planned to do to us reverberated in the dark sky as our prayers ascended to Heaven.

The first rocks crashed against the bus. Then suddenly the little boy's frightened voice turned to amazement.

"Grandpa, they've stopped!" he shouted. "Grandpa, they're running away! Look, Grandpa, look!"

Victor, Cissy and I straightened our trembling knees and peered at the incredible scene. The mob was running away; past the street light near the hotel, up the hill and into the street beyond.

With great relief we weakly thanked God for His protection. We didn't know whether we should *kill* JP when he finally returned for placing us in danger or be relieved that he could get us out of there.

The following Friday a few from the mob of teenagers were at our meeting point, but they were subdued and didn't try to intimidate the Nyoongar kids or abuse us. Although they were politely asked to join us they refused and backed away quietly.

Several weeks later I once again approached the mob and one young man, who looked frightened asked, "Who were those people you had at the bus that night we were going to smash you?" With a subdued voice he timidly continued, "We didn't see them until we were pretty close!" His eyes grew larger as he said, "They looked like soldiers standing on the roof of the bus. They wore shiny white clothes and they were armed! They really scared us!"

Although my hurried explanation of God's angelic protection was brief, the mob dispersed and never hassled us again.

1999

Friday afternoons before a weekend off are always busy because of packing clothes and food as well as organising pet care while away. But one particular Friday afternoon was more frantic than ever. It was the end of a week of flooding rains, where the nearby village of Glenreagh had been cut off by flood waters. Also, it was school holidays and there were extra visitors staying at Sherwood.

A stranger arrived in the early afternoon – a man in his late 20's, tall, rangy, blue eyes and long, wavy chestnut coloured hair. He asked if he could be shown around. He said that he was on holidays and was heading north when he took a deviation along Sherwood Creek Road (a strange deviation which is not always marked on maps and which had been cut by flood waters only 24 hours before).

As he drove past our gates he said that he had been curious about our sign and eventually turned around, four kilometres up the road. With rapt attention he listened to my usual explanation of the work and kept drawing me back to explain the basic purpose of Sherwood – to fulfil the will of Jesus Christ. He kept drawing me out to say the name of Jesus.

A phone call from a grieving parent interrupted our conversation, so Phyllis continued with the guided tour. Over afternoon tea on Milligan's verandah, he showed a keen interest in asking each person what he or she did at Sherwood. When he was asked what he did for work, he said that he was a waiter in private homes in Sydney.

Just before departing he asked if we had any literature on the work. As I walked him down to the office he asked if we received many phone calls from hurting people. When I answered "yes" he encouraged and affirmed me in that role (which I often *moan* about because of the emotional intensity and time factor). He took the Praise letters and once again affirmed and encouraged me in writing them so faithfully and diligently. His farewell handshake was warm and long and he once again affirmed me as a person as his piercing blue eyes looked into mine.

"What's your name?" I asked as he said goodbye.

"Michael," he replied.

Later, as I was taking dry clothes from the line I mused over that stranger's visit and wondered if we may have entertained an angel unawares. Hebrews 13:2 says *"Do not forget to entertain strangers, for by so doing, some people have entertained angels without knowing it."*

2001

Not all "angels" are as mysterious or elusive as they were in the first two stories – some "angels" are definitely flesh and blood.

Every seven years God miraculously provides for our family to visit JP's home country, Switzerland. In 2001 we only had three children who hadn't *flown the nest*. Although Kirstin was in year 12 it was still possible for her to accompany us for part of the time – which included her school holidays. With her good friend Kristle, we all enjoyed three weeks of wonderful hospitality reconnecting with family and friends.

Kirstin and Kristle were booked to fly out of Paris so I took them, plus Daniel and Melody to experience five days in that exciting city. After four days of cultural experiences where we visited cathedrals, monuments, saw the Mona Lisa and viewed Paris from the top of the Eiffel Tower for Melody's 10th birthday, they were "cultured out". So the final day was spent at Disney World.

The girls with their 'Airport Angels'

"Lord send an angel to watch over Kirstin and Kristle," I prayed as I slowly moved along the baggage queue at the airport. I was particularly concerned about their changeover in Bangkok to another airline.

In the milling throng I started up a conversation with a man who was similarly shuffling his bags forward. I found out he was Peter, from Australia; returning from Africa; worked voluntarily at a mission hospital; travelling with his wife; came from Nowra; on the same flight as the girls, including the changeover in Bangkok. To check out Peter's veracity I asked a final question. "Do you know Ray and June Dawson?" With an affirmative reply I knew that I was looking at my answer to prayer. Upon meeting Peter's wife Gloria, I knew that God had sent two 'angels' – not just one!

As my two beautiful, vivacious but naïve, teenage girls waved goodbye I knew that they would be safely chaperoned back to Australia. The other two children and I headed back to Switzerland by train with thankful hearts.

Chapter Fourteen

SHERWOOD GLEN

The Vision

Shortly after JP and I met in 1971, God imparted a vision to us – separately, yet the same vision. We were to set up a place where people who had been caught in the drug scene could come and have time to grow mentally, physically and spiritually. This place would be a witness to an unbelieving world and a doubting church that God is good. It was to be a faith work that relied totally on God to supply all our needs to further attest to His personal involvement.

The Fulfilment

After our marriage in 1972 God continued our preparation in WA. When it was the right time, God led us to a 56-hectare farm north of Coffs Harbour for which we were able to pay cash, through His miraculous provision.

In January 1978 the work began with a steady stream of drug addicts being housed in railway carriages. It was a steep learning curve filled with great joy, searing pain, racking disappointments, privation and hard physical work.

A Problem

The combination of men and women living and working closely together, inevitably led to physical attraction.

Relationships were formed and rehabilitation was forgotten! After five years we prayerfully closed the doors to single women and focused on single men and families.

Hints from Heaven

Over the next 20 years it was impossible to forget the needs of single women as every week calls were received from those in desperate circumstances.

Murder – Suicide

In February 1995 a distressed father visited Sherwood with his rebellious son. Tearfully the father pleaded for help. "Give me an application to keep the old man happy," the belligerent son said. "Drugs are too much fun at the moment. Maybe in twelve months I'll think about Sherwood".

Within days of this visit, the son, in a drug-fuelled psychosis brutally murdered his father. Shortly after, the Public Trustees notified JP that Sherwood was the beneficiary of the father's will as the son was not eligible to inherit. God planted a desire to dedicate any money from this Will to establish a women's rehab centre.

The wheels of justice turned slowly and four years later the son was deemed not guilty of murder, because, being under the influence of drugs he was not responsible for his actions. However, he was incarcerated in the psychiatric unit of Long Bay Jail for three years and Sherwood was now no longer eligible to receive his inheritance. Within a week of being released from jail the son committed suicide.

The Public Trustees once again notified Sherwood that because of the son's death we were the recipients of the original estate. Because of further legal complications the money, $255,000 was not deposited in the Sherwood account until seven years after the father's death.

The Location

Sherwood now had the financial means to help women and children so prayer for wisdom, leading and discernment were the course of action.

An unoccupied 232-hectare property nearby was where the Divine guidance led. It had never been cleared for farming but had been used to run cattle, to log, and to sand mine since white man's occupation in the previous century. Sandstone cliffs formed the eastern and western boundaries. A creek flowed through the valley and the Sherwood Nature Reserve fence line created the northern boundary. From the Sherwood Cliffs gate to the entrance of this property it was only 3½ kilometres – close enough to share resources but far enough away to avoid romances from marring rehabilitation (the "pheromone" barrier as JP called it).

At a Board meeting in September all aspects of the purchase of this land were being discussed when the vendor, *St...*, rang to say that our offer could not be accepted. When pushed to explain why he had gone against his promise, he said that it was in deference to his neighbours, the only other people living in the valley. They did not want a drug rehab next door to them. What a blow! We were so sure that this property was God's leading and He had already provided the money. Back to prayer!

The neighbours were approached but they had no intention of selling. They, *S & D*, and *St...* (the original vendor), were all told that God wanted Sherwood to set up a women's work in their valley. There was enough money to buy one or the other property – but not both. Neither wanted to sell!

All at Sherwood started praying that if God wanted us to buy both, then He would supply more money.

More Money

Eighteen months before this time, Sherwood had been contacted by another drug rehab further down the coast. They wanted advice as were struggling to function. It was a very difficult situation with many inherent obstacles. Some of their Board Members visited Sherwood to look for solutions, but eventually they decided to close the centre.

In December 2002 a phone call from a principal Member of the Board revealed that the place was on the market and Sherwood was to receive the majority of the money. Any charity, which folds up, must disperse of all assets to charities doing similar work. Sherwood received $450,000 at the exact time that we had been praying for enough money to buy both properties and to establish a women's work.

Money – Leading – but no Land

S & D were reminded that Sherwood still wanted to purchase land in the valley and now there was enough money to buy both blocks. They kindly, but firmly, said that they were not interested in selling as they loved their natural bush setting and home.

So, here it was at the end of 2002 with the leading from God where to locate the women's work, and the money to buy the land, but nothing was for sale.

Movement

In early January 2003 *St...*'s property was, once again up for sale and Sherwood was given the first option to purchase.

At a quickly convened Board meeting it was discovered that there was an access problem. The entrance to *St...*'s property required driving nine metres through the National Park, but they refused to grant permission for this access. The alternative was to travel 50 metres through *S & D's* land.

They would allow a verbal agreement but not give a written one. Without written legal access it was impossible to apply to council for a development application.

Because of the access delays, *St...* was threatening to put his property back on the open market. Sherwood's hands were tied legally, but not prayerfully.

Wonder Working Prayer

At the end of February, overwhelmed with frustration, JP requested that Sherwood pray. His specific instruction was for "God to bless *S&D* out of the valley".

One night in May *S & D* called to invite JP to discuss the possibility of selling. "We've had a change of circumstances in our life and we are ready to sell now." After negotiating a price within our range they settled on $292,000.

JP's curiosity couldn't be contained, so he asked as to the circumstances that brought on the change. They replied, "We are expecting a baby and *S* wants to be closer to town for the birth and the raising of the child." (*S & D* had been married for 16 years and this was to be their first baby).

After a stunned silence ,JP confessed that he might have had something to do with this pregnancy. Quickly, I said that he meant it figuratively and went on to explain about the prayer request for "God to bless them out of the valley".

Amidst our joyful laughter, *S* asked, "What did you have in mind? That we would win Tatts Lotto or something?" They were assured that there was no indication about how God would bless them. "You know how much we love it out here," *S* said. "This is the only reason we are selling".

The contracts for both properties were signed in July 2003 at a combined cost of $420,000 for 425 acres. By purchasing both properties, the whole valley, the problems of dissension with neighbours and legal access routes were solved.

Sherwood Glen

A great deal of thought and talk went into the choosing of a name for the property. "Sherwood Glen" was settled on as "Sherwood" maintains a link between the two ministries and "a glen" is a lightly wooded, small valley with a stream running through it. An apt description!

Sherwood Tobiah

In December 2003 *S & D's* baby boy was born and they called him Toby. This lovely name comes from the original Tobiyah meaning "God is good". With a slight adaptation we called the adjoining property "Sherwood Tobiah," to remind us of God's amazing provision.

Neither the Sherwood Tobiah house or *St...*'s rustic bush hut were suitable places to locate the women's work. The house was too close to the road to provide a secure environment and it wasn't surrounded by enough flat land for the multiple buildings required. The hut was in the middle of a sand mining quarry with scarred soil and vegetation. Not a pretty sight!

After much exploration a gently sloping area above the wetlands around the creek was chosen.

In early December a 33-ton excavator cleared two hectares on this site. As rural landowners we were eligible to clear this amount of land under the existing Government ruling. Also some of the sand-mining ravaged areas were restored, roads were built and a bridge over the creek was constructed.

A Good idea versus God's Idea

A local property developer offered us 12 cabins for free for removal, immediately. Was this an answer to our prayers for accommodation?

Our human logic wrestled with the possibilities – close location for removal, instant housing, awareness of opportunity, and free buildings! However, wise advice from our Board put a stop to this move. They pointed out the lack of good roads on Sherwood Glen for heavy transport vehicles, the lack of approval from Council for development, the difficulty of relocating the cabins, as they were built on concrete slabs, and the huge cost of clearing the site of these slabs.

Sadly we turned down the opportunity. But a great truth we have learned is: "A good idea is not necessarily God's idea".

Council Amalgamation

The Pristine Waters Council was in the throes of amalgamating into a mega, local government entity, the *Clarence Valley Council*. During the months of transition, the Council officials

Council staff visit

could not give definitive guidelines for the preparation of a development application. God-given experts helped JP prepare a DA e.g. surveyor, architect, solicitor and environmentalist. This was finally presented to the appropriate Council Official who received it with great hostility.

Twelve months had elapsed since the previous land clearing so a further two hectares were cleared on the future development site. Because of the horrific Canberra bush fires the Rural Fire Service now required an 80-metre exclusion zone from houses to bush. This extra clearing would fulfil their ordinance.

Incorporation

With the proposed women's rehab on a separate property we needed to expand our structural operation by becoming incorporated. Thanks to the diligence of one of our Board Members, a mentor and dear friend, John Smith, we re-wrote our constitution to fulfil incorporation guidelines.

The Power Who Is vs The Powers That Be

Prayerfully, but not always patiently, Sherwood waited for the Council's approval of the Development Application for the Glen. Any communication received was very negative, with threats of fines and/or jail for the land clearing. "Don't spend any more time or money because your D.A. won't be approved as Council's road and your access roads are sub-standard," came the dire warning.

Finally an official delegation from Council inspected Sherwood Glen. They were very unhappy about the clearing of four hectares and said that it was an illegal act as this was not under the rural provision with a development proposal of this magnitude. "But it's done now! You would never have been given permission for the clearing if you had made proper application," they stated through gritted teeth.

They inspected the cleared land, bridge, dams, road, area pegged out for buildings and distance from the bush. After hearing about God's miraculous provision of the place through a murder, suicide and baby they began to thaw. A visit to Sherwood Cliffs revealed to them a rehab in action with its structure and organisation, and further clarified the new development to the Council delegates.

After a gruelling 12 months wait the DA was finally approved in early December – with 84 conditions!

When JP went to Grafton to have some of the perplexing conditions explained the official leaned over his desk and snarled, "Can't you read! What it says, it says!" Holding his fingers close together he continued, "You have no idea, it was <u>this</u> close to getting the whole thing knocked on the head. It wasn't my decision!"

After the Blessing the Battle Continues

Now that the Development Application had been approved, Building Applications were submitted to the Council. No house construction could commence until the approval was received. However, a shed could be built without this permission so preparations for the 2006 Mobile Mission Maintenance's annual visit were made.

Flooding rains knocked the access bridge's footings so that it was not safe for vehicles – let alone trucks loaded with heavy building materials. The only other access to the Glen site was via a rough, fire trail. As the water dried up and the trail was improved with culverts, pipes and fill, the MMM team spent their first week demolishing a church hall in Woolgoolga.

Finally, the concrete trucks were able to do the delivery and 25 energetic and enthusiastic MMMers set to work. By the end of their third week the shed was completed – the first building at the women's rehab.

Builder Needed

At the end of 2004 JP and I moved to *Sherwood Tobiah*. This was a Divinely inspired and Divinely provided move. We were now in a position to oversee both ministries and leave the daily management to others.

Roger and Julie Ward came to work at Sherwood with the desire to build the new facility for women, but their role changed when they took over the management position. Roger's experience as NSW team leader for MMM equipped him for leadership but he had to now share the building of Sherwood Glen with another. God inspired a Victorian couple to spend many months every year travelling north to supervise, tile, build, paint and work in every area of construction. Alan and Bronwyn Ronalds answered the call and diligently served.

Aggressive Prayer

Although the DA had been approved we still couldn't commence construction until the Building Application was approved.

In March 2007 Charlie praised God loudly when the Council rang to acknowledge that they had found the missing engineer's report – lost in their office for eight weeks. He had, just that morning, been aggressive in prayer regarding the constant delays.

We oscillated between wondering if Satan was hindering the work, or if God was refining us for the task. Satan may be mighty, but God is ALMIGHTY!

Council still required more engineering details before they would approve the Building Application.

Temptation

Meanwhile, we were offered increasingly larger amounts of money (up to triple the original purchase price) for Sherwood Tobiah. The money sounded good but then we could have the future rehab jeopardized by disgruntled neighbours. The temptation to sell was resisted.

The Limit of the Possible

Three and a half years after the original Building Application was presented to Council it was finally approved on May 23rd 2007 – Praise the Lord!

Seven cabins, three staff homes and a multi-purpose central building had been approved for construction. Sherwood Glen could finally begin to be built!

The frustrations and faith of the past years were best described by Oswald Chambers – *"God can do nothing for me until I get to the limit of the possible."*

JP flew to Sydney to personally receive a $16,000 cheque from the Ryde Baptist Church – money they had sacrificially raised toward the first cabin.

Dedication

Part of the 2008 celebrations for Sherwood's 30 years of ministry included a dedication of Sherwood Glen. Over 200 people inspected the buildings in progress – two cabins and one staff house – then gathered for the official speeches, prayer and praise.

Coffs Harbour State Member of Parliament, Andrew Fraser, included these words in his impassioned speech, "… If there is a message here today, it is that God is on this bloke's side!"

Charlie struggled to hold back tears as he spoke of the hassles of gaining official approval to commence building.

He assured us of the potential the place had to continue the transforming work that had been manifested at Sherwood over 30 years. With JP's encouraging hand on his shoulder, Charlie tearfully thanked God for the past provision, the present support and the future miracles of transformed lives.

Andrew Fraser MP, Luke Hartsuyker MP, JP & Steve Cansdell MP

Steady Progress

Over the next two years, Allen and Bronwyn made regular trips back to Sherwood. During Allen's visits God brought many other tradesmen along eg carpenters, electricians, plasterers, plumbers, painters, builders, bricklayers and labourers.

Roger steadily exercised his building gifts and incorporated the talents of the staff and seekers. Building teams from all over the state targeted specific projects. MMM work parties came annually to push along the construction. Local *tradies* put up roofs, dug trenches and made kitchens.

A needed architectural plan was divinely procured when a visiting couple "just happened" to visit three days after our Board requested it. A "chance" mention of the need of this

3D profile prompted the visitor to offer to do it, as he was a builder and structural engineer. Three weeks after their visit the beautifully drawn plans arrived by email. `

Skulduggery

In 1984 the local Lions Club supplied three truckloads of bricks and flooring timber for the construction of the dining room at Sherwood Cliffs.

The then president of the Club, Alan Scolari, had maintained a keen interest in this work and was pleased to hear that we were expanding. "Although I'm in my 80's now I want to see *Lions* being part of the new place," he said. Numerous phone calls, documentation of company and charity status, Council approval paperwork, site plans etc. were given to Alan as he laboriously presented a submission.

In response, the Pacific City Coffs Harbour Lions Club members raised $20,000. Spurred on by their support he gained another $15,000 from the Australian Lions Foundation. Not to be deterred by the mountain of paperwork required, Alan successfully presented the need to the Lions Club

International Foundation USA who doubled the total already raised.

In total seventy thousand dollars had been raised for the construction of one cabin.

We are very thankful for the interest and generosity of so many people in the wider community.

In October 2010 the money was officially presented by Alan, who was familiar with the Sherwood faith and budgeting strategies. He said, "This $70,000 was originally intended to build one unit, however with careful budgeting and the use of volunteer labour, the team at Sherwood were able to build three units. No doubt some skulduggery was used!"

An Army of Volunteers

Once a date was set for the opening of the women's rehab an army of volunteers offered their time and talents.

An ex-seeker from the south coast arrived with his tip-truck and bobcat to do the landscaping around the building. Truckloads of plants from a failed housing project in Coffs were soon in the ground. The house paddock was drained; sand, soil, mulch and compost were trucked in; paths were marked out, formed up and concreted in to place; the saw millers had to work hard to meet the demands of the fencing team.

By opening day a camellia had produced its first delicate pink bloom.

Opening Day

On Saturday May 7th 2011 over 400 excited supporters marvelled at the progress, the facilities and the future. They trod the paths, leaned on the fences and walked through the buildings. Our local politicians pledged their support as we gathered under the shady marquees.

The beautiful bouquets prompted my speech. I compared the flowers with the ladies who would come to Sherwood Glen for help. There would be the *self-contained* banksias, *prickly* grass-tree spikes, *showy* antirrhinums, *delicate* orchids, *twisted* tortured willows etc. but all are precious and together they make a beautiful bouquet in the hands of a skilled artisan.

Staff

The first staff, Dennis and Eva Munton, moved into one of the cabins in August 2010. With frost on the ground outside they suffered the hardships of pioneering without electricity (the solar power was yet to be connected) and heating.

Dennis & Eva Munton

Colin and Chantal Kemsley and their four children were the next staff God called to the Glen. After three years at Sherwood Cliffs they moved down in January.

Although the buildings were up, the new staff needed to establish the structure of the rehab. Whereas the men's rehab revolved around a vocational emphasis the women had a core need for relational issues to be central. Policies and protocols needed to be developed and documented so that both rehabs could work under the same structural umbrella – yet allow for the gender differences. Chantal was greatly helped by a new staff member, Marion White, who had prepared such documentation guidelines in her work as an Occupational Therapist in Western Australia.

Kemsley family

Seekers

The ladies started arriving in mid 2011 and sure enough, they lived up to my analogy of flowers in a bouquet. Some were *delicate*, some *prickly*, some *tortured* and *self-contained* and some *showy*. But all were warmly received and respectfully integrated into the Sherwood family.

Life in rehab. isn't easy! Hopefully this time allows the opportunity to detox from the drugs of abuse, de-clutter the mind, settle the anxiety, rebuild a healthy body, understand controlling issues, set boundaries, restore relationships, sort out legal problems and plan a new direction. Addressing all of these issues goes a long way to safeguarding a drug free future. But we believe that having the person *unavailable* to the drugs is where true freedom is found. Something greater needs to replace the lesser! Being born-again as a new person, where the old ways are put to death and where new and right ways emerge, brings a life change that sustains. Drugs will always be available in our society but a person can be unavailable to them when Jesus Christ reigns in their life.

Operating

Over the next three years steady improvements were made to the establishment eg carports with art, linen and pantry rooms, fireplaces installed, outdoor eating area constructed, water tanks fitted onto each building, a back-up generator for the solar power and a small bus purchased. God faithfully met all of these needs through His generous, listening people.

But best of all, was the opportunity to receive and care for beautiful women whose lives had been damaged by sin and circumstances.

Caretaker Mode

After Kemsley's seven years of service they took a well-deserved sabbatical of three months to travel around Australia. On their return they felt that they should move from Sherwood Glen to take over the management of Sherwood Cliffs. Without the necessary strong leadership the Glen could no longer take women. Therefore it was placed in caretaker mode with a capable resident, Dave Boylan, maintaining it in tip-top shape.

As I write it is still in *holding-mode*. When I walk around the eerily quiet place I could become overwhelmed by a spirit of resignation and defeat. However I choose to remember the incredible journey that we have experienced in the establishment of the Glen. Then my praise rises heavenward... and His peace descends. A deep assurance replaces the doubts. Nothing in God's economy is ever wasted.

Today our prayers are for: peace to wait upon Him, provision of the right staff, and power from His Holy Spirit to glorify Jesus in this time.

COUNTLESS
God's Timing

If there is something we have learned in our journey with Christ over 40 years it is – *the timing is as important as the leading.* Psalm 31:15 says, *"MY TIMES ARE IN YOUR HANDS" (NIV).* This is often easier said than done!

The preceding verse says *"BUT I TRUST IN YOU O LORD; I SAY 'YOU ARE MY GOD'".* It takes a supernatural empowering to truly acknowledge God's timing and to step out of our natural constraints of time. We see a need and want to offer help immediately. God also knows the need but He has a much bigger view of the problem and the solution.

During the waiting period faith is exercised. We seek God as never before; the desperation doesn't hide God, but reveals Him as we come to the end of our own resources and our ability to manipulate circumstances. It stresses us – but it also stretches us! The lesson learned is that God can be trusted. And the final assurance is, *"YOU ARE MY GOD!"*

Chapter Fifteen

ANIMAL ANTICS

1981-82

Sherwood runs beef and dairy cattle to utilise the farm's grass and to supplement the food needs. Mostly, the cattle graze quietly in the background but one playful bull made a lasting impression.

"How did that huge rock get into the middle of the road?" queried JP. Two men jumped out of the bus and rolled the offending rock to the side of the road. Everyone had been in town for the day so the question had no logical answer.

A few days later the rock appeared again, on the road – followed by a large stump sometime after that. The blockages were removed requiring the brute strength of two or three men. The mystery continued. Finally, the culprit was spotted! There was the bull, shifting the boulder back onto the road by pushing it along with his hard head.

His antics continued to everyone's amusement...but one day his playful behaviour could have had expensive ramifications.

Work was progressing on reassembling the old school house that had been transported from Taree. Stan Goodwin, an 80-year-old from the south coast, offered his carpentry skills for the project. He stayed in a house at Sherwood and drove his yellow mini minor car up to the work site each morning. He parked in the open paddock and unfolded his tall, thin frame out of the tiny car.

One day, as they were working, someone glanced up and called out, "Hey, look at the bull! Its putting its shoulder to Stan's mini, ready to roll it down into the gully!"

The *Sherwood bulldozer* was foiled in his attempt and Stan no longer parked in the paddock.

1983

At morning devotions Russell prayed for a milking cow as the present milker was drying up. This request was recorded in the Prayer and Praise Diary...and was heard in Heaven!

During morning tea, JP received a phone call from a local dairyman who said that he had a cow and calf for Sherwood. JP excitedly told all present and assigned Charlie to take the truck and pick up the animals from Upper Orara.

A sceptical seeker made sure he went on the truck as he was certain that JP had rigged this "answer to prayer". While Charlie loaded up the animals, the seeker took the farmer aside. "When did JP ring you about Sherwood's need for another milking cow?" he asked. With a twinkle in his blue eyes, the farmer said that he hadn't talked to JP for months.

"Well, why did you ring him?" the perplexed seeker asked.

"When I was busy milking this morning I felt God tell me to give Sherwood a cow," the farmer replied. "One of my favourite cows was no longer producing enough milk for a commercial situation but she still had a good number of years in her. So, as soon as I finished milking, I gave JP a ring."

JP milking, 1980

This incident not only planted seeds of belief in God's existence in that seeker, but also into others who have heard the story.

1984

During the Christmas break when the dining room was not used, something strange was happening. Each morning there was a strong smell of urine, and animal fur on the tables. I was the only one with cats so I apologised profusely and disinfected the area. Even though I diligently locked the cats inside our house at night, each morning there was the same disgusting smell and sight.

The mystery was eventually solved – and my cats were not to blame!

The other end of the dining carriage contained the popular table tennis room. Over the past year, in the excitement of the game, large holes had been kicked into the fibro panels below the windows. Table tennis balls inevitably landed into these holes and the players had to feel around in the dark cavities, to retrieve them.

When Russell pulled the broken panels off the wall, he made on interesting discovery. A sleepy one and a half metre carpet snake (python) was not pleased to be disturbed. It's cosy home smelled of urine and was littered with animal fur from quiet meals. It was amazing that no one had felt the snake when they plunged their hand into the cavity in search of the lost balls.

My cats were exonerated, the snake was removed, the holes were repaired and the dining room remained clean.

1999

One evening, a distressed seeker went for a walk down to the paddock. As anxious emotions threatened to overwhelm, he lay down in the grass and curled up into a ball to wallow in his misery.

Three inquisitive calves investigated the interloper in their grass. Tentatively they sniffed him all over. Then they softly licked his hair, arms and face. This gentle ministry broke through the self-imposed barriers and the seeker cried out, "God have mercy on me and forgive me."

Several days later, a similar thing happened to another seeker. This time God used a cow to minister to the hurting soul.

Many times we have seen domestic pets soothe and comfort people but it is wonderful to know that God can also use farm animals, as well as native creatures - *'all creatures great and small."*

Skippy listening to Ashlee reading a Skippy story

2007

While mowing behind the houses, Mike observed a life and death battle.

A one and a half metre long red-belly black snake was slithering along a rock wall in an agitated manner. Suddenly, it darted into a hole between the rocks, with only its tail protruding. The snake then writhed and wriggled furiously as it backed out of the hole. A 20cm bluetongue lizard was firmly clamped over the snake's mouth. No matter how many gyrations the snake performed, the lizard would not let go. Eventually the little lizard released its grip...and the snake fled.

Mike told this story at evening devotions and finished with the lesson learned – *NEVER GIVE UP!*

Animals abound at Sherwood, but snakes are the most bothersome, so let's finish this chapter with yet another snake story.

2010

Imagine 5 women, 2 children and 1 dog alone on the isolated Sherwood Glen property – with an over-friendly, persistent two-metre long carpet snake (python). Although they are not poisonous, they are easily able to strangle small animals and birds...and they are scary!

A frightened scream rent the air! A seeker lady screamed that a snake was going under her cabin. Quickly the other women devised a strategy to deflect its course. However the snake determinedly slithered toward the safety and protection of the cabin.

Then they had another idea! They grabbed a 4-metre long drainpipe and guided the snake into it. The pipe was then picked up, run across the yard and thrown over the fence. But this was not far enough away!

The pipe was then picked up again (before the confused snake could escape) and speedily carried to the top of the hill and into the bush. The women breathed a sigh of relief.

But...the next morning the snake had returned. This time it was in the chook house, only 30 cm from a clucky hen.

Once again, the women implemented a team strategy and managed to pull the snake out of the chook house and shove it into a feedbag – Phew!

As the girls were heading up to Sherwood Cliffs they planned to drop the snake off into the bush, half way between the two properties and far enough away from easy meals of chickens. But after the excitement of the drama, they only remembered the snake when they arrived at the gate.

No-one ever mentioned a new two metre snake joining the crew at Sherwood so maybe it decided to keep well away from interfering humans and headed into the bush for peace and quiet.

Chapter Sixteen

DANGER

1994

After four years of receiving half the annual rainfall, Sherwood was under drought declaration. In such extreme conditions only one spark was needed to start a bushfire.

In January, Sydney had been ravaged by bushfire but on the north coast it wasn't until late September that the extreme conditions turned dangerous here.

October was filled with searing heat and the ever-present smoke smudged the horizon and dimmed the sky.

On Tuesday the 8th November we were notified to prepare for evacuation as a bushfire was spreading dangerously close. Each person packed a small bag, protection measures were instigated, less flammable clothing was worn and then we gathered for prayer. As Lyn prayed for the fire to turn on itself, we all felt that this was the way for us all to pray.

A deep peace settled upon us, even though the air was so thick with smoke that the cliffs on the other side of the valley were completely obliterated. The children nervously returned to school in the afternoon, but returned at 3pm singing at the top of their lungs the words of Geoff Bullock's song, 'Shelter', proclaiming the peace, comfort and shelter that only God gives in times of stress.

Their teacher, Bindy, had encouraged them to sing their praises to God and said that, "the louder you sing the more the devil hates it."

The fire did turn on itself and head away from Sherwood, but it didn't go out! As the week progressed news reports alerted us that the fire was still a threat. Falling ash, smoke and a surveillance helicopter which flew low over us at least five times a day, reinforced that there was danger close by. A friend in Glenreagh who was volunteering at the Fire Station, heard the firemen discussing the grimness of the situation. "I don't think we can save Sherwood Cliffs," a fireman worriedly said. She quickly responded, "No, they'll be right – the place is blessed – it belongs to the Lord."

Waiting for the fire to arrive!

By Friday afternoon, the top of the cliff was alight and small fires were burning in the rainforest only 30 metres from the houses. It was too late to evacuate! A total of eight fire units from all around the State, and a grader to cut firebreaks, were present at Sherwood on Friday night (approximately 80 personnel).

An eerie evening darkness descended with waterfall-like cascades of fire dropping from the blazing cliff top. Ledges of brightly burning vegetation emphasised the towering threat.

Danger

The rainforest at the bottom of the cliff was well alight, with the flickering flames glowing against the sandstone. Many huge trees were alight, but the most spectacular and dangerous was a 50m high gum tree burning fiercely only 40m from the houses.

Our prayer was that this tree would not fall toward the houses. Peaceful expectation of God's protection overrode fear, so we sat on deck chairs in the middle of the lawn and the pyjama-clad children lay on the trampolines to watch the pyrotechnic display. After 3 hours the massive tree fell! The top 15 metres crumbled first in an explosive roar. Like a fire-breathing dragon the remaining 35m belched thick smoke and cinders high into the air. Finally, the centre of the trunk burst open and the two sides scissored on themselves and crashed straight down to the earth. With a great sense of relief and praise, we wearily headed off to bed at 10.30pm.

All night the firemen continued cutting a firebreak through the bush toward the highway.

In the early morning light I was amazed to see that there was still some green vegetation alive in the rainforest. Some of the massive old trees had gone, but not a cinder or a spark, not a toppling tree or a burning branch had crossed the narrow dirt track behind the houses. Although the water pipes had melted, the fibreglass water tank on a cliff ledge, and surrounded by trees, was not damaged.

Some Christian friends had prayed on Friday morning that God would put a hedge around Sherwood, that the angels would blow the fire back and the trees would drop on themselves. Truly, their prayers were answered!

Six weeks later, on Christmas day, we woke to receive the best Christmas present ever – the sound of steady rain falling on the roof. Almost 100mls (four inches) fell in two days, replenishing our drought-ravaged land, refreshing our drought-weary souls. A local newspaper called the rain, "A DIVINE GIFT".

2007

One Monday afternoon, Georgie drove up the Sherwood driveway to see five young men smashing the welcoming two "old blokes" (life size painted figures) at the front gate. They were pulling them out of the ground with a rope hooked to their vehicle. As she approached, they quickly hid their faces and sped off, but not before she got their number plate, description of their vehicle and details of them.

Less than a month later they returned in the middle of the night to repeat their destruction. But this time they put the rope around the gates and caused the brick walls to fracture and the iron gates to buckle. Twelve thousand dollars worth of damage was sustained.

This was not an isolated incident of vandalism in the district. A bus shelter was destroyed 10kms up the road that same night, using the same tactic. Private and police investigation revealed the identity of the perpetrators, but prosecution has not been possible. No doubt these young men will continue in their crimes, growing even more dangerous in their activities. Our prayer is that, for the sake of their souls, and for society, they will have their sins revealed.

Thankfully a very skilled metal worker who had been in the Sherwood program was able to restore the twisted buckled gates. A former staffer who is a bricklayer was able to reconstruct the walls to their former glory. The "Burly Gates" have been restored.

Office break-in

2011

On the 4th December we returned home from Church to a state of utter chaos in the main office. During our six hour absence thieves had ransacked the office, broken into both safes and stolen all the contents. Oxy-acetylene equipment and grinders from the Sherwood workshop were abandoned amongst the scattered papers. It was a mind-numbing sight!

The use of our own cutting equipment, and even the knowledge of the location of a new disk for the grinder, pointed to an inside job. Someone who knew our movements, the location of the office and safes, as well as the equipment available, indicated first-hand information. Only some blurred fingerprints on a fire extinguisher were found, as the thieves wore gloves.

Along with the seeker's money was Sherwood cash that had been set aside for Christmas holidays, vehicles registrations, emergency expenses, and for a variety of other costs associated with the construction of Sherwood Glen.

They even took a little cash box that JP's father had given him 45 years ago and had held his birth certificate and both his Australian and Swiss passports. Other important documentation was also stolen.

We had to furnish the police with names and details of all the people who would have had an intimate knowledge of the workshop equipment over the past few years – staff, seekers and visitors. Police investigation so far has been unsuccessful.

"It must have been junkies as they were only after money and saleable things like passports," one investigator surmised. "The fact that they didn't trash the rest of the place, burn down the buildings, steal electronic equipment or vehicles shows that they just wanted cash," he continued.

"They didn't damage JP's motorbike when they used it as a step ladder to climb through the window which they smashed to enter the office, so they must have an affinity with bikes."

The police, and our connections with the "underworld" (through seekers from that background), may not have solved this disaster, but, we have a greater investigative power at work – the "over world". He who is above all, is aware of the whole situation. We are His precious children, "the apple of His eye" and this violation will not go unpunished. Rather than let our imaginations and accusations run rife, we put our trust in Jesus – the Son of God. Whether the money is returned or not, our prayer is for justice; that the thieves will come under conviction that will lead to their conversion. From darkness to light! From evil to good! Isaiah 42:3 states *"In faithfullness he will bring forth justice."(NIV)*.

Many people shared their concerns for our situation, beseeched Heaven with their prayers and blessed us with money to help replace the losses. One person wrote, *"My Pastor gave me your newsletter at a Bible study yesterday and I read about the break-in. Here's $20 to help you get back on your feet again"*. Another letter came bearing these words and containing $1,000. *"Just to bring a smile on your face and a song in your heart! Is everything settled after the theft? How can you fail? He/they must have been desperate but known with the facility. God bless you and keep you!"*

Truly God does bless us and keep us. He is our ever-present help in times of trouble.

Chapter Seventeen

HEAL THE SICK – RAISE THE DEAD

Between the time that God gave us the vision to run a rehab in 1971, and it becoming a reality in 1978, we were on a steep learning curve: Learning to trust God in and for everything. When Jesus sent His disciples out to preach His message that *the kingdom of heaven is near,* they had seen His power to heal the sick and raise the dead.

We had no trouble believing that, but seeing a man proudly waving his signed death certificate in the air grew our faith in Jesus' ongoing ability to conquer death. Ray Roberts shared his remarkable story at our youth group in our home in Perth and I have included a condensed version of the story in this book.

We believe that Jesus can heal today and our expectant prayer is *"May Your will be done."* We do not demand that our will be done but leave it in His sovereign hands.

1975

Ray and Rita Roberts had retired from the WA mission fields to work as caretakers in the Blue Mountains of NSW at a Christian campsite. One Friday evening Ray was putting the finishing touches to the highest point of the roof in the auditorium. Just as he reached out to the unpainted spot, the ladder broke and he fell 10 metres onto his back – severing his spinal cord and crushing vertebrae. Although Ray lived through this accident he became a quadriplegic, with limited head movement and spent a great deal of time in the ex-servicemen's hospital, Concord, in Sydney.

Ray lingered for years in his deteriorating, haggard body. He did not want to die in hospital, so when his "end" was near he was taken home to be lovingly tended by his wife Rita.

One Saturday morning, Rita called the doctor as Ray was in a distressed state with his eyes staring, great beads of sweat on his brow and breathing terribly. The doctor arrived 20 minutes later just as Ray gave his last death gurgle.

After doing a thorough examination the doctor kindly said, "Mrs Roberts, Ray has passed into the presence of the Lord. He won't have to suffer anymore."

When Ray's body was taken to the local morgue, Rita was comforted by her neighbours. They knelt down and thanked God that Ray was free from his suffering. As they prayed, they felt as though they were being lifted up on wings and they were filled with a joyous ecstasy.

Because Ray had died at home an autopsy was standard procedure. When the doctor examined the body he thought he saw a sign of life and immediately called in the doctor who had signed the death certificate. He noted that Ray had vomited up some large chunks of black blood and transferred him to a hospital bed. He ordered that Ray should receive no medication as he would only linger a little while from the stroke he had suffered.

On Sunday Ray was moved back to Concord Hospital and on Tuesday he woke up! Without thinking, Ray lifted his hand to tidy his dishevelled hair.

"The Lord has restored my hand," he thought. As Ray looked out the hospital window he said that everything looked extra green. He remembered leaving his body and going to Heaven but that there was no human way to describe what it was like.

"The light was completely different to any light I had seen on earth," Ray said. "It was beautiful singing that was better than all the choirs and orchestras on earth. The Lord came and talked to me."

"Ray you have to go back. I have more work for you to do," He said.

"No Lord," Ray pleaded. "I want to stay. It's so beautiful here."

"Ray" the Lord said. "I have more work for you to do and on Friday you will be going home."

Ray woke with these words ringing in his ears on Tuesday. Over the next few days every doctor in the place hovered around Ray's bed and examined the results of brain scans and x-rays. Ray's broken spine had been healed, the stroke had caused no damage and his blood group had changed from the original "O" type to now an "A" type.

"I felt like a guinea pig," Ray said. When the chief neurosurgeon called in, Ray said, "I wish you would tell these guys that I'm going home today," as he indicated the encircling doctors.

"Oh yes," he replied. "You can if you want to."

Half an hour later Ray had a visitor who said, "I'm the ambulance man who brought your body down to Concord on Sunday. I've heard about you and I thought that I would pop in and see how you are going."

"No," Ray excitedly replied. "The Lord sent you to take me home."

Halfway home in the ambulance, Ray said that he saw a beautiful rainbow and he was suddenly aware that the Lord had completely healed him.

Outside his home he resisted the ambulance driver's help. "You carried me out, but, I'm going to walk in," he confidently said. Ray had told God that he would give this first year of his new life to the Aboriginal people. For many years they had asked Ray to return to the West and said that they were praying for him to preach to them again. This was impossible with his quadriplegia, but now, all things were possible.

Ray laboured for the Lord for 15 years and proudly showed everyone his signed death certificate. Everywhere he went people praised God for His miraculous restoration of this man – from death to life, from illness to health.

1987

While visiting family in Switzerland a desperate woman pleaded with JP to pray for her as she had been diagnosed with throat cancer. He was so busy that he couldn't meet up with her. Daily she called as the diagnosis was confirmed with biopsies and surgery was scheduled.

Finally, it was God's time to perform His signs and wonders. JP said, "I put both my hands across the table, held hers and I just asked the Lord to touch her throat and heal her."

"Strangely, at that very moment when I felt I should pray, I had a real calm come over me. All the other times I just didn't feel like praying."

Two days later she rang and said, "I went to the hospital for my scheduled surgery yesterday. The doctors had only made a small incision in my throat when they discovered a pocket of fat – a lypoma." With the biopsy results before them, they quickly checked to see if they had the right patient. The biopsy showed a positive cancerous growth but the incision revealed fatty tissues. She was totally healed from that cancer and is still living a healthy life thirty years later.

1987

During that same trip to Switzerland God showed His loving kindness through healing a three-year-old boy.

The distraught parents had to immediately respond to their son's coughing at night as he couldn't stop until he vomited. They had to quickly lay him on his side so he wouldn't choke. Neurologists couldn't determine the cause of the coughing and were testing for a type of brain seizure.

JP was at their home one evening when he saw the distressing situation and was touched by their worry. "Have you prayed over him?" JP asked.

The parents had not realized that Jesus still heals today so JP showed them James 5:12 in the Bible where it says that if anyone is sick you should call the elders and anoint the person with oil. Armed with salad oil, the only oil available, they went upstairs to pray over the sleeping child. JP said, "I felt very strongly that God would heal that night. We knelt around his bed and I prayed over the little fellow and anointed his head with oil. I rebuked the sickness in Jesus' name and asked the Lord to show His favour by healing him. The little boy gave a little shudder and a big sigh of relief. He took a deep breath and kept on sleeping."

The next day the parents rang to ask if they should keep the specialist's appointment in Zurich at the end of the week.

"Would it indicate a lack of faith if we do?" they queried.

"No, just go," JP replied confidently as he sensed that God had healed the child and this would be confirmation. The tests were better than normal and there were no abnormalities found. Now, thirty years later, he has grown into a healthy young man who has never had any relapse of the fitting from the day that JP felt led to pray for him.

We give God the glory!

1990

Georgie's daughter, Bethany, grew up at Sherwood and excelled at horse riding. After finishing a degree at Sydney University she now lives in the heart of the city with her wonderful husband, Caleb. However, it did not look like Bethany's life would turn out so well when she was born.

Her father refused all responsibility for Bethany straight after her birth and Georgie was forced to leave her home and marriage. They came to Sherwood to stay with Georgie's father Charlie Quarmby who was grieving the loss of his beautiful wife of 47 years, Jean.

Two heart-broken adults should have had the joy of a baby to ease their pain, but this was not the case, as, Bethany experienced many health issues.

She was born with a cataract on the lens of her left eye. This should have been diagnosed at birth and operated on straight away, but it was overlooked. A month after her birth she was seen by a paediatrician in Coffs Harbour for other life-threatening health issues and he noticed the cataract straight away. Bethany was immediately flown down to the Camperdown Children's Hospital for the removal of the cataract. Time was of the essence as the longer the cataract blocked Bethany's vision, the more sight she was losing in her left eye.

The day of the operation came and the clouded lens was removed. Georgie said ,"I thought that was the end of the problem. Little did I know the trauma that was to follow." Bethany had to have a contact lens inserted into her left eye and her right eye patched for part of every day. Putting that contact lens in was a repeated traumatic experience for mother and baby.

A lovely orthoptist, Anne, was given the job of training Georgie for the task. Even Anne, and her assistant, took 15 minutes to get the lens in. Bethany brushed it out of her eye the first night so Georgie went again and again to learn the art of inserting the lens. Although Bethany was only five weeks old she struggled and screamed during the whole procedure. Georgie was extremely fragile as a new mother with a distressed, ill baby, a broken marriage, the sudden death of her own mother and her father facing a serious operation in the midst of his own grief.

One day Anne came to introduce another orthoptist who was taking over Bethany's care. Anne explained that she was moving back to her hometown – Coffs Harbour! Georgie said, "It was nothing short of a miracle as time and time again I had to drive into Coffs to Anne so that she could help me put the lens into Bethany's eye."

It also just happened that there was a Seeker lady, Lorraine, who had worked with an eye specialist in North Sydney. One day when Georgie had reached the end of her endurance with putting in the lens she was out walking with Bethany in the pram. Lorraine quietly sidled alongside and very quietly spoke. "Don't give up mate, she is not going to remember all this and will thank you when she is a teenager." Quietly she moved on, but Georgie said, "It was like an angel had spoken deep into my spirit and I continued on with the battle with Lorraine's quiet encouragement."

2002

As Christians we are not immune from pain and suffering, but in it, we are not alone as Jesus promises that He will never leave us or forsake us. Like Paul, who pleaded with God to remove his thorn in the flesh, we too have come to the conclusion that difficulties such as weakness, hardship, insults, persecution, keep us desperate for Him. We cling tightly to Jesus and it is His strength that holds us.

In an ice-skating accident JP sustained a deep cut to his elbow which became seriously infected. Two courses of antibiotics eventually quelled the infection but while his immune system was compromised he was bitten by about 50 ticks.

Shortly afterwards, I noticed that he was over-reacting to stressful situations. He was anxious about answering the phone and intense counselling situations. He was constantly tired, his mind was racing and he would wake unrefreshed. He lacked energy and was exhausted by the simplest tasks.

During this time, two loyal co-workers stood beside JP. Henk and Geoff were like Aaron and Hur who held Moses' weary arms up in the air while the battle raged.

After numerous medical tests, our doctor (a canny Scot) gave JP a firm, fatherly talk.

"You have done too much for too long! You are not as young as you think you are. You have to slow down and delegate more."

This was the same advice given to Moses, and now JP had to hand over some of his greatest stressors – particularly the phone. Each morning following the staff meeting he would crawl back into bed for an hour to rest his weary body and to refresh his soul by listening to the Bible on cassette tape.

As well as delegating stressful situations, JP began to rattle with all the natural food supplements he was taking. A daily jog with the dog, going to bed early and being covered in prayer from all over Australia helped keep him from going over the edge. Although he was still looking for physiological factors, he had placed himself in the hands of our merciful Lord Jesus.

I knew that JP had stepped back from the edge when, one Sunday afternoon, he spent two hours in intense counselling with a new seeker couple. Their emotions were raw, their minds twisted and their withdrawals painful, but still JP lovingly talked and talked and talked. They left comforted, and although he was physically tired, he was not exhausted.

Three months into this time of travail, JP took our motor home into Coffs Harbour for ten days. He relaxed, slept, socialised, prayed and then rested some more. It was a time for him to refocus and pray.

Meanwhile at Sherwood a spiritual warfare team prayed against any spiritual attacks on him and on the work.

Everyone and everything was placed under the blood of Jesus Christ.

The day he returned there was frenetic activity at Sherwood – a cousin was visiting, a phone company was investigating the connection of a new phone system and he brought back a new staff member. That night JP fell into bed tired, but not exhausted. Praise God, he had now turned his back on the edge.

Whether the traumatic three months were the result of a demonic attack, a mid-life crisis, the empty (emptying) nest syndrome, the skating injuries, the ticks or whatever, we thank God that we don't have to understand everything in order to trust Him. Praise the Lord, anyway and in every way!

A couple of months later JP was invited to a men's breakfast in Perth with a group of young Baptist pastors. As they bared their souls and shared their disappointments, frustrations and pain in their churches he listened with true compassion. Instead of responding with his usual *"WALK ON WATER FAITH"* he could feel their pain. He could comfort them with the assurance of Jesus – who will never leave them or forsake them.

Jesus said, *"My grace is sufficient for you, for my power is made perfect in weakness."* 2 Corinthians 12:9 (NIV)

2004 - written by Roger and Julie Ward

Back in November 2001, Roger was blessed to receive the life-giving donation of a kidney from his older brother. At the time, we were working for MMM and enjoyed annual work parties to Sherwood Cliffs. With the freedom from dialysis we desired to serve the Lord in a greater capacity. Not sure what that would look like we decided to seek the Lord. Julie went to Africa on a short-term mission and Roger went to Hillsong Conference. Whilst Africa had many great needs and opportunities it was very clearly not the place for a transplant recipient as at the time AIDS was rampant and hospital facilities limited. Almost jokingly we said, "What about Sherwood Cliffs?" They were advertising for a teacher, for which Julie qualified, and the possibility of building a new facility for women required someone with building experience, for which Roger qualified.

It was decided that a quick reconnaissance visit was in order. Jessica was coming to the end of her primary education and we were in a dilemma as to which high school to send her to. We loved Northcross, a lovely little Christian Community School where she was school captain, but could not settle on the next step. So, on our journey to find out if Sherwood would be our next step Jessica came along. We had the necessary interviews while Jess experienced the wonderful farm life so loved by Sherwood kids. By the end of the weekend she told us that she didn't mind what we decided, she was coming to Sherwood Cliffs! Coffs Harbour Christian Community School opened its doors and Jess enjoyed the dedicated and committed teaching of its staff for her entire secondary schooling.

There were many other obstacles still to get around. Some of them were physical, like the kangaroo we nearly hit and the fallen tree across the road on our way to Sherwood, but many of them were a little more serious. Despite Roger's new kidney there was still the consideration of regular medical check-ups to ensure there were no rejection episodes. Whilst Coffs Harbour had an excellent dialysis unit there was not a permanent renal specialist. Patients had to rely on a visiting nephrologist once a month flying in from Sydney.

Roger was under the supervision of Royal North Shore Hospital in Sydney. The Renal Registrar who attended him was a young overseas doctor working to gain the qualifications required to practice in Australia. He and his family moved into the street adjacent to the MMM centre where we lived and his three daughters attended the Christian school where our daughter Jessica was enrolled. We would often meet at the traffic lights as we walked our children to school. Imagine our surprise when we told each other we were moving to Coffs Harbour. The Registrar, now able to practice as a specialist, was starting up a Renal Clinic and Roger was one of his first patients.

That medical relationship was to extend over the nearly ten years we were at Sherwood. We were made aware of how important that personal, local attention was when Roger had to have his appendix removed. The renal physician was on hand to care for the grafted organ while the other was removed. A fly-in, fly-out doctor would have had to rely on telephone diagnosis or Roger would have needed to be transferred. The friendly, efficient regular check-ups were a constant reminder of God's faithful provision.

Chapter Eighteen

REVELATIONS TO UNBELIEVERS

1987

A disgruntled, generous donor tried three times to destroy the work of Sherwood when he was not given a leadership position. His final act of sabotage was to report us to the Charities Division of the Australian Tax Office for fraud.

Two officious auditors trolled through our accounts for three days, even refusing a cup of tea in case it could be considered bribery. Demands to explain the receipt and nature of gifts received for ten years was a harrowing experience. However, the overflowing book full of itemised receipts satisfied every enquiry.

"How do we know you aren't pocketing cash donations?" one auditor demanded. Our prayer for patience for JP was answered when he firmly replied, "Listen mate, I answer to a higher power than the ATO. He wouldn't bless us if I was stealing from the work."

As though to prove the point, God orchestrated that a battered, stained envelope should arrive in the mail that very day. It was addressed to JP and contained four $50 notes – but there was no indication of the sender. As JP shook some red dust out of the envelope, he held up the money and explained that this situation was not uncommon.

The flummoxed ATO officials deliberated over whether it was meant for Sherwood or for JP.

"When in doubt, I give it to the Lord," JP calmly said. "But in this case I know who the money comes from! It's from my mate, Scotty, who works in the Kimberley scratching around some gold leases. A couple of times a year he sends such a donation. Although there is no note or return address, and the envelope is addressed to me, I know that he wants it to be used for the ministry". The auditors clucked over this unprofessional protocol and JP continued, "There are far better ways to get rich than running a drug rehab for ten years. I'm certainly not in this for the money!"

Finally the ATO officials visited our accountant in Coffs Harbour to substantiate the annual audits. Then, they finished up with a visit to the Baptist Church to verify that the complicated lease-rent arrangement was adhered to. In order to tithe all of Sherwood's income, a Christian solicitor had drawn up a lease-rent arrangement, so that all money received could be tithed and distributed to other missions through the church. Therefore the lease-rent enabled us to direct 10% of our income to others.

After talking to Pastor Don Kemsley, one official wearily scratched his head and said, "I came up to Sherwood Cliffs as an atheist. I'm leaving as an agnostic!"

1986

In July, a young, troubled man caught the train from Sydney but disappeared along the way.

Late October, a staff family was in Taree. They visited the local Church of Christ and were introduced, from the pulpit, as coming from Sherwood Cliffs. After the service a young man introduced himself to them and said ,"I'm the missing seeker! I've spent a miserable few months and I just happened to be passing through Taree when I felt that I should go to a church. I haven't been inside a church for five years!"

Russell and Sue knew that this was more than just a coincidence. Being assured that he was now ready to commit to rehab they took the young man back to Sherwood.

1989

One day, while JP was working in the main office, Telecom technicians were doing routine maintenance in the nearby office. JP received a phone call from an ex-seeker who was threatening to commit suicide. JP talked with this man for over 20 minutes in a loud voice, reminding him of his worth to God and that life can have meaning and hope. The distraught caller's replies echoed loudly around the room.

After a successful conclusion to the call, one of the workmen quizzed JP about the work at Sherwood. "Do you get a lot of these calls?" he asked. With a nonchalant shrug JP replied, "Often! They're quite a common occurrence".

The Telecom man then said, "Well, I don't give much for your religion but I see that you're doing a good job. I can't see why Telecom can't do something for you."

A few weeks later this man rang and said, "I've spoken to many Telecom officials and they've agreed to install a brand new *Commander Ten* telephone system throughout Sherwood Cliffs, free of charge."

JP praised God, as this was the very system he had investigated, and decided against, because it was too expensive.

The following Saturday, three Telecom workers installed the system between all the houses. When their boss heard that they had worked on their day off, he insisted that the Company pay their wages for the day's work.

Chapter Nineteen

BABIES - A LABOUR OF LOVE

1972

Even as young Christians we believed that Jesus is interested in all aspects of our life and will answer all our prayers – according to His will, not ours.

When a young couple from Germany met us in Derby we invited them to stay at the United Aboriginal Mission where we were working. Their car had broken down and they had to wait for a week for gearbox parts to arrive from Perth.

Although they were antagonistic toward the gospel message, they appreciated the friendly, free accommodation. As JP is a motor mechanic he helped with the repairs.

The two men had pulled the gearbox out of the car and used a 44-gallon drum as a workbench. Unknown to them, a small washer that was a gearbox spacer-bearing fell into the bin and before they realised its loss, the drum was sent to the rubbish tip.

Without that washer the gearbox could not be repaired. Due to Derby's isolation there was none available in that dusty Kimberley town and a delivery from Perth (1,000 kms south) would take another week.

"Let's pray," JP eagerly said. "Jesus you know where that washer is!" In their desperation the young couple was open to prayer.

Babies - A Labour of Love

Straight after praying, JP said they should go to the tip to find the washer. Although the couple was unsure of this enthusiastic *mad man* they were soon scratching around amongst the piles of rubbish.

"Thank you Lord," JP yelled as he exultantly held up the missing part. "I knew you would show us where it was."

The car was soon fixed but the couple was hesitant to leave. Finally, they asked if we would pray for them. They had been married for a few years and they had not been able to have children.

Realising that the finding of the washer was merely an introduction to the existence of a loving God, we eagerly prayed together with them. "Continue the good work that you have started Lord," we prayed as we waved them farewell.

A year later a beautiful card arrived in the mail. The picture on the front showed two birds on a branch with a little one in the middle!

Daniel Walker, first baby born at Sherwood, 1978

We don't know if they went on to find a saving relationship with Jesus but we do know that He performed two miracles for them in dusty Derby.

1980

Charlie and Jean Quarmby had no sooner arrived at Sherwood to work, when we told them that God had miraculously provided for us to fly to Switzerland the following year. Even though they assured us that they were willing to *hold the fort*, we had another concern. Our second child was due to arrive during that visit.

Trusting God for the timing of the birth and the extra expenses for the hospitalisation, we excitedly caught up with JP's family. Two-year-old Luke met his grandparents and saw snow for the first time. We revelled in the love and relaxed in the freedom of being away from the intensity of life in a drug rehab.

With our departure dates already booked we were very pleased when Marcus arrived two weeks early and not two weeks late!

When we landed in Sydney, anxious hours were forcibly spent in a restricted area of the airport trying to prove that Marcus was actually our baby. He had not been correctly registered at the Consulate in Berne so we were suspected of kidnapping and smuggling. As phone calls traversed the globe to verify our claim, I adamantly refused to be parted from my baby. Finally we were allowed to enter Australia. But, only after promising to officially correct Marcus' legal immigrant status within the week. What a homecoming!

1988

A regular visitor to Sherwood was a dear friend from WA, Effie Duke, who came for six weeks every two years. She bounced in with overflowing joy in the Lord to encourage seekers and staff alike. On every visit she was asked to share her miracle stories and, although the following incident occurred years before, I have included it here as this is when

I recorded it more fully for the previous Sherwood book, *"FAITH WORKS IN CHRIST"*.

"...During my time in the air force in WW11 I became very sick and was taken to the Force's Hospital in Perth. After a ten hour operation the doctor told me that he had removed a football-sized cyst which had completely encased all of my reproductive organs and part of my bowel. "The good news is that you are alive," he said. "But the bad news is that you will never be able to have children and you will never be strong".

When the war ended I married my husband, Wilf, and we decided to adopt children. A medical certificate was required to prove that it was impossible for me to have children before we could adopt our two boys.

Our little family lived and worked in Northam...until the Lord called us to work at an Aboriginal Mission in Norseman.

On February 6th, three years later, we had just returned from our Christmas holidays and I was standing at the kitchen sink when God spoke to me.

"Effie, I'm going to give you a baby daughter," He said. I was so amazed that I sat back and said, "Lord you can't. I haven't got anything to have children with. Why, it's 18 years since I had that operation and I'm in my 40's. You can't."

All in a quandary I thought, *Who could I tell who wouldn't think that I'd gone crazy?* I ran next door to Ray and Rita Roberts as they loved the Lord with all their hearts and every breath in their bodies.

"Rita, the Lord just told me that He's going to give me a baby daughter," I blurted out.

Without turning a hair she said, "Did you say Thank you Lord?"

"No, I said you'll have to prove it to me Lord."

"Let's say thank you now," Rita kindly said. So we knelt together in her kitchen and I said, "Lord, thank you. But I still can't believe it."

After a while it became obvious that I was going to have a baby, so I went to the young doctor in Norseman.

"What symptoms do you have?" he enquired. Never having menstruated since my total hysterectomy I had to admit that I didn't have any symptoms, but that God had told me.

The look on the doctor's face revealed that he thought I was crazy, but he calmly said, "We need something more concrete than that Mrs Duke."

He took blood and ten days later the results came back positive.

"You'll have to go to Perth," the flummoxed doctor exclaimed. "I won't have anything to do with the delivery in this little country hospital with no extra medical help!"

I never had one day of sickness and I was able to care for the Aboriginal children and our two boys the whole time.

When I was 43 years old I gave birth to our healthy and beautiful daughter, Debbie. She was born by caesarean section and it was noted that she had attached herself to my bowel.

Only God could have worked a miracle like that. God certainly does love to bless His people.

1996

A young couple, Kees and Alice, excitedly awaited the birth of their first child. This is part of Kees' account of Josiah's birth.

"On Sunday the 18th August at 18.05 our son Josiah was born. It was a traumatic experience for him and for us as new parents.

After a long, 20-hour labour, Josiah was born with birth trauma causing him to be lethargic, irritable and not breathing. The cord around his neck could have played a part in this, as well as the duration of the birth. The doctor tried to revive Josiah with oxygen and an alarm signal was sent to the Special Care Nursery. Specialised staff came running in and took the baby...

Alice said, "I'm OK. Quickly Kees go after him." I prayed as four people worked on Josiah with the oxygen and testing equipment. Suddenly I felt a coldness and fear in the room and instantly the Lord reminded me what to do.

I stepped back and said (in a loud voice), "In the name of Jesus, you spirits of fear and death get out of here!"

As those words were spoken, fear left and Josiah responded to the oxygen mask, by breathing by himself – slowly at first, but stronger and stronger as the minutes progressed. The paediatrician was honest with us, saying that the lack of oxygen could have damaged his brain. Josiah had no control over his left arm...That night I opened my Bible and read Psalm 30:5b (NKJV) which says that..."Weeping may endure for a night, but joy cometh in the morning..." What a promise!

That night Alice read Psalm 41:2-3 (NIV) "The Lord will protect him and preserve his life; he will bless him and not surrender him to the desire of his foes. The Lord will sustain him on his sickbed and restore him from his bed of illness."

The next morning I went to the hospital and saw that Josiah's left arm and other body parts were fully responding to the tests. The doctor was amazed as many things progressed in the first few days of his life – his fever left and the swelling on his head disappeared...

Three months later Kees wrote:

"Josiah is doing really well now. The paediatrician calls him a miracle baby and is amazed that there is no brain damage or other effects from the difficult birth...

Praise the Lord!

2007

I don't think that I had ever prayed for an overdue baby NOT to arrive before, but on Monday 20th August, I certainly did. Increasing falls of rain over the weekend, after 50 days without a drop falling, escalated with a torrential downpour all night.

On Tuesday we woke to the news that Sherwood was an island – cut off by floodwaters in every direction.

Chantal was almost a week overdue with her third baby but thankfully exhibiting no signs of labour. To be on the safe side I notified the ambulance service and they assured me that they could have a helicopter from Lismore to her in an hour. Finally the rain eased and the floodwaters dropped enough in one direction to transport Chantal out by 4-wheel drive on the Tuesday afternoon. On Thursday morning she and Colin welcomed the arrival of their son, Cyrus Eli, in the safety of the hospital. Cyrus is Sherwood baby number 17.

2009

Jake and Shiralee Butterman wrote of the birth of their sons and I will quote part of their account.

"On 25th September a double blessing arrived in Sydney (7 weeks early) – healthy sons, Ezra Joel (1800gms) and Seth Asher (1500gms). With 8 ambulances, over a dozen humidicribs, including more than 15 doctors, nurses and ambo's...the twins were transported from Sydney to Coffs Harbour, only for us to endure another hectic couple of weeks, travelling back and forth from Sherwood to the Hospital. After a very exhausting month we finally have our family together.

"...We thank our Lord Jesus Christ who has entrusted us with His gift of children. Our children are a 'heritage from the Lord', the fruit

of the womb, 'arrows in the hands of a warrior'. 'Blessed is the man whose quiver is full of them' (Psalm 127:3-5 NIV)

2003

The story of Sherwood Glen is told elsewhere in this book but a re-iteration of a miraculous baby boy needs to be included in this chapter.

God had given us the direction for a women's rehab, provided the money and shown us the actual property. However there was a major stumbling block, which could only be moved by God.

One day in late February we started praying that God *would bless a neighbouring couple out of the valley* so we could purchase their adjoining land to the future rehab. But they were adamant that they had no intention to ever sell their new home.

One night in May we received a call to say that they wanted to discuss the possibility of selling. "We've had a change of circumstances in our life and we need to sell now," they said.

After settling on a price JP's curiosity couldn't be contained so he asked as to the circumstances that brought on this change of mind.

"We are expecting a baby," they replied (after 16 years of marriage they were now to be blessed with their first child). We laughed and we cried when we heard the news. We praised God for His miraculous hand in this whole situation.

Because they sold their land to us, then we were able to go ahead and purchase the future Sherwood Glen.

2012

Our grandchild number 12's imminent arrival was "pacified" with my words – "she won't be born before midnight as there's a lot more hard labour ahead. She's two weeks early and she's a first child." How wrong was I. Chantal had driven only a little south of Glenreagh when Mel's baby arrived. As Chantal pulled off the road Mel was already cradling Marli's head. The rest of her quickly followed as Chantal caught her in her outstretched hands.

By the time I arrived the local First Responders were on the scene to cut the cord. Mel was stunned at the speed of the delivery and Chantal was congratulated for her cool head. As we waited for the ambulance I had time for a good look and a big cuddle of Amarlia Ellen.

2012

We were eagerly looking forward to welcoming another grandchild into our earthly family. But instead, God had other plans and He welcomed Billy Kemsley into our heavenly family.

Chantal and Colin wrote:

"We had hoped to be sharing the exciting news of another Kemsley on the way. Sadly our precious Billy bypassed this home and headed straight for glory. Born on the 18th October, weighing a tiny 190 grams and just 25 cm in length.

"Saturated in sadness, yet filled with a peace, we said our goodbyes confident we will meet again."

2017

As I finished writing this chapter on "Babies" I have included Sherwood's latest little addition.

Five years to the day since Billy Kemsley was born and welcomed into the waiting arms of Jesus, her little sister arrived. Although it was a difficult birth for both mother and baby we thank God for an experienced obstetrician and an amazing health system in Australia.

Two Sherwood babies arrived this year – making numbers 23 and 24 on the list of 40 years. Freya Ellery was born in August and Honi Blossom Kemsley came in October. What a loving community these two little girls will be immersed in as they grow up together.

Thank you Lord!

Chapter Twenty

OF DEATH AND DYING

2017

In July the family gathered at the front of the Church to sadly watch my mother's coffin being carried out by six grandsons as pallbearers.

As the hearse slowly pulled out of the driveway, JP raised one hand in the air and loudly called out *"SEE YOU LATER MUM!"*

The tension was broken and tears flowed freely. JP had just spoken at Mum's funeral about Jesus. "He was either a liar, a lunatic or the Son of God," he said. "If Jesus was a liar, then don't believe what He spoke! If Jesus was a lunatic, then keep away from Him! But if he is the Son of God, as He claimed, then you have to respond to Him."

We have responded and have been immersed in a loving relationship with Jesus. We believe Him when He said that, *"In my Father's house are many rooms... I am going there to prepare a place for you"* (John 14: 2-4 NIV). We believe that He willingly allowed Himself to be crucified, that He triumphantly conquered death and was seen by hundreds of witnesses – alive and well.

Our faith in Jesus assures us of a life everlasting. It comforts our souls, wipes away our tears and causes death to lose its sting. This assurance has empowered us to handle the deaths of many people over the 40 years of Sherwood's ministry.

1980

A pastor, caught in the grip of drug addiction, spent a few days at Sherwood. Although his life was a mess he insisted on leaving. On his way north, he crashed his car and was killed.

A pall of sadness and failure hung heavily on us when we heard the news. "Could we have done better?" "Should we have tried harder?" Our doubts and confusion were eased when an old saint shared a strange Bible verse with us, saying *"sometimes God allows the destruction of the body for the salvation of the soul."* His parphrase of 1 Corinthians 5:5.

The struggle for sobriety, the madness of addiction, and the defeat of sin was annihilated with his death. He had now entered into Heaven where he was safe in the arms of Jesus.

That verse and the Giver of that verse, was to comfort us in many similar situations in the years ahead.

1990

Jean Quarmby went off to Sydney in early February in high spirits to face a hip replacement operation. Although this surgery was successful, complications set in and she did not regain consciousness from a burst aneurysm. She unstintingly shared herself with so many and had a profound influence on all the women at Sherwood in the ten years she served Jesus here. A few memories spring to mind:

Fresh scones for morning tea; clambering up the cliff face in search of her wayward dachshund dog; motivating everyone for a game of tennis or a bushwalk; bravely swinging off the rope swing in Glenreagh and landing in the river below; tending her beautiful garden; turning mountains of cucumbers into delicious pickles; enjoying a swim at the beach almost every Sunday; walking up to dinner, holding hands, with her precious husband Charlie; going into Coffs

Harbour on the night before her departure for Sydney, to encourage a young family in distress.

Inhibited by the demands of young children and the constancy of ministry, I used my morning shower as a time to cry tears of sadness at Jean's death. About six weeks later I felt God speak to me, *"You are no longer crying for Jean,"* He said. *"You are crying for yourself!"*

Instantly, the truth of these words struck home and I repented of my self-pity. I asked for strength to guide the women's aspect of Sherwood. For ten years, Jean and I had been a team and I often hid behind her maturity as I tended four babies.

Jean's death following surgery was very fresh in our minds when Charlie received word that a hospital bed was available for him to have his worn out hip replaced. We were worried at the prospect, but Charlie wisely consoled us with the assurance that if the operation was not successful then he would be with Jean in the presence of the Lord. If it was successful then he would have less pain, greater movement... and still be with us.

Three weeks before Charlie's operation, his daughter Georgie's little baby, Bethany Jean, started having strange *turns* and it was later discovered that she was impaired in one eye by a cataract.

Sue, Pam and I prayed about who should accompany Georgie and Charlie to Sydney. Sue "won" and stayed with Phyllis Richmond at Manly. They drove from one hospital to the other to comfort and care for all three of these precious people. Bethany's cataract was removed on Wednesday and Charlie had his operation on Friday. It was a traumatic week of fluctuating fear and faith, but both operations were successful.

1994

Every seven years God has miraculously provided for us to reconnect with family and friends in Switzerland.

As we were busily preparing for our departure in 1994, we received the terrible news that Daniel and Melody's mother had died of a drug overdose in Sydney. These special children had spent a great deal of time in our home in the previous two years as their widowed mother battled her *demons*. I quickly flew to Sydney and was greeted by two traumatized little orphans. As seven-year-old Daniel hugged me tightly he said with absolute confidence, "I now have a younger father and an older mother, two more sisters and two more brothers."

Thankfully Debbie had always told the children that they would have our family to turn to if anything should happen to her. She also had a Power of Attorney drawn up by a solicitor expressing her wish that we exercise custody, care and control over her children's future.

Weighed down by concern and responsibility I pleaded with God about our imminent departure for Switzerland and thus, abandoning the children in their time of great need. I was flooded with a deep peace when I heard God comfort me with *"Not only was Debbie's death in my hands, but the timing of her death also."*

Eleven days later we tearfully farewelled Daniel and two year old Melody, knowing that they would be ensconced in their mother's family and lovingly cared for by them all.

1995

Sitting next to me at morning tea was a very sick man whose health had deteriorated from 25 years of drug abuse. Two years before, he had spent five weeks at Sherwood, but didn't want to stay any longer. Then be began telephoning again, pleading with us to have him back, as he said, "the drugs are killing me!"

When he did arrive he was *stoned* from having been on a weeklong heroin binge to celebrate his acceptance into rehab. He spent the first few days in a confused, weakened state.

Recognizing that his symptoms were more than just a tough withdrawal on an older body, we asked a Christian doctor to come out to Sherwood to assess the situation. His diagnosis prompted the seeker's immediate transfer to hospital and a dire warning to us that he doubted if he would survive. "I have never seen these symptoms in real life," the doctor said. "Only in textbooks!"

The seeker's lovely Scottish mother immediately flew up from Sydney to be with her son in intensive care. His estranged wife and children visited and made peace with him although he was unconscious. A week later the seeker died in hospital from endocarditis – a major infection to the heart valves that was introduced to his body through dirty needles when injecting heroin.

1997

Jack came to us as a seeker in 1984, badly damaged from alcohol abuse. His doctor said that, "Jack was a *bushy* from way back and it would be cruel to put him in a city retirement facility. He'll be lucky to last two years," the doctor predicted as we accepted him into the program. The 'years that the locusts had eaten' were restored to Jack and eventually he stayed on at Sherwood as part of the family.

Twelve years later Jack's abdominal pain was finally diagnosed as inoperable cancer. He did not want to die in hospital and God fulfilled his desire to remain at Sherwood by providing wonderful palliative care nurses who visited regularly. Also new staff members, Andre and Priska Ott were well prepared for this task. Priska was a registered nurse and Andre had grown up in a home where his widowed mother cared for the dying in her home-hospice.

Jack continued to chop wood and dig gardens. Although we tried hiding the axes, we would hear the sound of chopping when he used his own hidden axe. The medication kept him relatively pain free and he even enjoyed a family holiday with us to the Kimberley in WA in his last year of life.

Jack's dying made a big impact on our son Daniel, as he had a realistic fear of death from being present when both of his natural parents died. Daniel spent a lot of time with Jack and found comfort in Jack's stoic suffering and calm assurance.

In April, Jack passed into eternity here at Sherwood, in the arms of Andre. Jack's battle with cancer was over. The primary schoolers all had time to say their good byes, especially Daniel, before they went into Coffs Harbour for their fortnightly time at *big school*. The undertakers had removed Jack's body before they returned home.

Charlie and JP took the funeral service, which was a very special tribute to a much-loved man. When Jack died his fridge was still full of chocolates so JP invited all the children who had ever received chocolates from Mr Jack to come forward. About 40 children – from two year old to 19 year olds – filed past Jack's coffin, which was adorned with his axe, hat and potatoes. Those 40 would have been one third of the recipients of Mr Jack's kindness over thirteen years.

Brushing tears from my eyes, I dug Georgie in the ribs and whispered that she should join the queue as she, too, had often availed herself of Mr Jack's chocolates when the *munchies* hit.

2014

After 36 years of running a drug rehab, JP and I came to the end of ourselves. Was it time to quit and close the doors?

Our bodies are ageing even though our spirits are willing. In 2014 we pushed through one of our hardest periods. God had warned us at the start of the year that this would be a time of CONSECRATION and a time to WATCH AND WAIT. We survived, but we came to the end of ourselves and realised that if we didn't step aside and handover the work to others, then the vision would die with us!

The pain of knowing that five ex-seekers had died since Christmas added to the heaviness of the year. Their "early" deaths caused us grief, but also in a perverse way, brought a quiet peace. In spite of the circumstances and timing of these deaths there is a certainty of their Saviour's redeeming sacrifice. Each one had committed himself to Jesus during their "short" earthly lives and it is God's promise to *present us before His glorious presence without fault and with great joy…*

Even before we accepted the reality of our fallibility, God was raising up others to carry on. Not to just carry it on as we did, but to carry if further into the future. The Kemsleys have been God-ordained, God-equipped and God-prepared for *JUST SUCH A TIME AS THIS!*

2017

This chapter commenced with a brief account of my mother's (Joan Hughes) funeral a month ago.

Last weekend we celebrated her life at a memorial service in her hometown of Manilla NSW. This was a special time to round off Mum's life with family and old friends. Some of her ashes will go into the memorial wall at the cemetery next to my father's and the rest of her ashes we scattered into the Namoi River. The sadness of parting remains but the joy of a life well lived remains. *Oh death, where is your sting?*

"In Africa, when a young person dies we grieve. But when an old person dies, we rejoice." I was comforted with these words from a dear friend as we were preparing for Mum's funeral.

Chapter Twentyone

WHAT'S NEXT?

"What's your succession plan for Sherwood?" we are often asked. Sometimes it is a bold, demanding question. At other times, it is asked in a hesitant manner in case it might offend us to be reminded of our eventual demise.

As we immersed ourselves in the never ending stream of needy people, this question niggled in our minds too. Usually the thoughts arose in the middle of the night when physical activity had ceased and the head had time to catch up. Before the thoughts could overwhelm with strategies, doubts or fears they were handed to God in prayer. After all Sherwood was His work, and He holds the future. Little did we know that He was speaking into the hearts of a young couple in 2007...and this is their story.

2007

"Hi there! We're the new staff, the Kemsleys. We have just started here at Sherwood Cliffs two weeks ago.

I, Chantal, was a Reifler (JP and Honi's daughter). I grew up at Sherwood and spent the first 18 years of my life here.

I, Colin, was born in Coffs Harbour and moved from place to place about every 18 months. We lived in Christian communities in Tahlee Bible College and on the mission field in the Solomon Islands, as well as with my grandparents Don and Margaret Kemsley.

As a teenager I rejected my Godly inheritance and made some very wrong decisions which led to substance abuse, broken relationships, and ultimately separation from my Creator.

It was the anguished cry from my Mother that made me see the light and call out to God.

I ran to Sherwood Cliffs and looked to God for answers. He restored and renewed me mentally and physically. If I had one answer to how I broke free from my drug addiction, then it would be God. Without a doubt! Sure it took willpower, effort and strength to hold onto Him. But, He held me tighter!

Chantal continues…

Colin and I married in 2001…and somehow we always thought that we would come and work at Sherwood. But, we always thought that it would be years from now. Obviously God had other plans.

At the end of last year (2006) Colin graduated from university after studying Technology Education (Design and Technology) for four years. He applied for jobs nationally, but didn't get any positive responses. By mid-March we were both wondering why God still had us in Coffs Harbour and why did we both feel it wasn't where we were meant to be?

So we began to pray and search for what it was that God wanted us to be doing and where it was. Unbeknown to each other we both felt that we were being called to Sherwood. When we both finally talked about what we were feeling (after about four weeks) we were shocked to discover that we had the same feelings and thoughts. Sherwood – and soon!

It was another two weeks before we mentioned things to Mum and Dad. We asked for lots of prayer from them, as well as from some other significant people. We wanted to know that it was the right thing and the right time. After only a week, it was official. Yes, they all thought, and now! We would start in a month.

For three years Colin and Chantal worked together with a strong team around them. Some excerpts from their Praise Letter contributions describe this time.

2008

"It is so exciting to be able to see God at work in changing lives, including our own...It is not always comfortable or easy and we can react in many different ways but, praise God, He provides the strength."

Later in the year Chantal wrote:

"Life at Sherwood is always the same, but it is always changing. The physical tasks are the same, but it's the people and their lives who are constantly changing.

"For someone like me who gets bored very easily, it is great to have so much diversity among the people to keep me occupied. It works well for us both as Colin loves the security of the routine."

2010

"The past few months have been a busy time for Colin and I as we have been filling in for Roger and Julie Ward as second in charge. The Wards are away for three months on their Sabbatical – long service leave."

This stint of leadership was God's preparation for the Kemsley's to move on – 5kms down the road, to establish the rehab program at Sherwood Glen.

2011

"We've been busy down here setting up cabins, finishing off the houses, building fences, a vegetable garden and a chook pen...Colin is enjoying these opportunities to learn new things and put into practice many of the things he learnt at Sherwood Cliffs.

"As we focus on getting all the 'little' things done, our driving force behind this is our excitement and anticipation for things to come. We're praying that God will open the doors when He is ready and then the women will come."

Over the next three years the ladies and their children did come to be offered restoration. The Kemsleys and other caring staff reached out in love to provide security, healthy living instruction and role modelling, all the time revealing Jesus.

During the busyness of rehab Chantal was taking our *wing and a prayer* experiences and was systematically compiling clear documentation. With the help of another staff member, Marion White who had worked as an Occupational Therapist with WA health, they collated our methods. Eventually, policies and protocols were on paper and could be handed onto future workers.

2015

In the previous year JP and I pushed on through one of our hardest periods. Our bodies are ageing even though our spirits are willing. We survived the year, but we came to the end of ourselves and realised that if we didn't step aside and hand-over, then the vision would die with us. Even before we accepted this reality, God was raising up others to carry on. Not just to carry it on as we did, but to carry it further into the future.

Colin and Chantal have taken over the management of the rehab while JP and I have moved into directorship roles. The transition period will, no doubt, have its trials for all concerned, but we know it is God's direction.

The two key goals for Sherwood remain the same:

- To trust God for everything (e.g. healing, wisdom, strength, staff, finances etc.) so that Sherwood is a witness to an unbelieving world and a doubting church that He is good and He is able.
- To see lives changed for Eternity.

Chantal and Colin bring a wealth of personal experiences. They have been on staff for 7 years where, for four of those years they pioneered the women's rehab program at Sherwood Glen.

There are some new things that they plan to implement such as:

- Structured support and guidance for staff.
- Bringing a more outward focus to the local and church community.
- Working with seekers on a more personal level through directed goal planning and group studies sessions.

All three of these strategies have commenced with an amazing structuring of each week – rosters designate who, when, where, what and why! Unexpected situations have not interrupted outcomes although flexibility and grace are paramount for success.

2016

A year down the track Chantal wrote:

"For those of you that are thinking, 'And just how is JP handling ALL this change?' Let me assure you that it is in God's hands. One thing that JP is, he is faithful in listening to God whether he likes what he hears or not. He has been the least of our problems. No, we don't butt heads. Surprisingly to many we actually work well together. Yes, he has his quirks, but don't we all. It's just that our quirks make sense to us and we can fall into the trap of believing that we are the only ones without them. No, we are not secretly hoping that they will retire and move far away. We are far from ready to take on the responsibility of running Sherwood on our own. We have a lot to learn and what better people to learn from, than from those who have been before us. At times it can be an unpredictable and exhilarating ride when JP is at the wheel but one thing you can always trust is that it won't be dull or boring. Thank you for your faithful support.

"Last month marked nine years at Sherwood for our family. The time seems to have just disappeared but then we look at the kids; 2 more than we arrived, we think of our age; we're not in our twenties anymore, we reflect on the many people that have crossed our path since being here: staff, seekers, volunteers and the many guests, we think of the diversity of tasks that we have done and the skills we have learnt along the way.

"And suddenly nine years doesn't seem long at all. Actually it seems quite the contrary, how on earth have we fitted so much into our time here? As we reminisce about our life at Sherwood we remembered the highs and the lows, the good and the bad, the bearable and the seemingly unbearable, the mighty hand of God and the unimaginably incomprehensible horrific work of man. Through it all God is faithful and He is the only place where we can truly find solace. Sometimes the obstacles seem to get bigger and harder, but each year seems to get easier and more enjoyable. We truly do love living here, we love the community, we love the heart of the place and we love the variety of His creation."

2017 Sherwood Staff family

Our mission is to
    refresh the weary,
    refocus the lost,
    rebuild the broken.

Our heart is to
    see God changing lives for eternity.

SHERWOOD CHRISTIAN REHAB CENTRE
P O BOX 2
GLENREAGH NSW 2450
AUSTRALIA
    Phone 02 66 492139
    info@sherwoodcliffs.com.au
    www.sherwoodcliffs.com.au

SHERWOOD DRUG AND ALCOHOL REHABILITATION CENTRE

A Christian Community established in 1978, Sherwood is the realisation of a vision God gave John Pierre (JP) and Honi Reifler.

In 1971 they felt God burdening them to provide a place for those struggling with addiction. A place for them to have time to grow physically, mentally and spiritually.

LOCATION

Both centres are situated on Sherwood Creek Road, in the Sherwood valley, 3km apart and approximately 10 minutes east of Glenreagh, NSW, Australia (50 minutes drive from Coffs Harbour).

OUR CENTRES

The Sherwood Rehab Centres are staffed by full time volunteers who live on site at both properties and are committed to the needs of those participating in the program. Volunteers are essential to the functioning and running of all aspects of the organisation and the programs provided. Our family orientated program of rehabilitation is an expression of our holistic concern for people.

Primary schooling is available from Kindergarten to Year 6 at the Sherwood School situated on the Sherwood Cliffs property and is available to the children living at either centre. This is a satellite school of Coffs Harbour Christian Community School.

SHERWOOD CLIFFS

This is the original site developed in 1978 and caters for single men and married couples with up to 4 children. Sherwood Cliffs is a farm that provides a substantial amount of produce for both centres. The program revolves heavily around an active work routine that is farm orientated.

SHERWOOD GLEN

This caters for single women and single mothers with up to 3 children. Sherwood Glen is a small farm that has enough gardens and poultry to supplement the daily diet. A large proportion of the program revolves around an active work routine focusing on garden and yard maintenance. At present this facility is not operating.

HOW WE LIVE

At the Sherwood Rehabs we live together, work together and share together. Each person residing on a Sherwood property is encouraged to participate in all aspects of the community life, including meal times, work programs and outings.

We aim to provide a family environment where unconditional love and acceptance is evident, where family relationships are re-developed and where wider support networks are developed to enable a smooth transition to living in the wider community once a person or family has completed their rehabilitation.

"We loved you so much that we were delighted to share with you not only the gospel of God but our lives as well." 1 Thessalonians 2:8 (NIV)

OUR PROGRAM

Hidden, but not hiding in this tranquil environment, is an atmosphere of love, honest work and practical Christianity. People seeking change have an opportunity to find real answers to their needs.

We are a residential rehabilitation centre with our program running from 6-12 months, depending on the needs of the individual.

The Sherwood program encourages a healthy lifestyle involving an active work routine, regular exercise and the re-establishment of good sleep routines.

Aspects of the program include:

- Daily group sessions,
- Vocational training
- Social and Recreational opportunities
- Studies on recovery and personal growth
- Involvement with the wider community.

We aim to provide a balanced program that covers all dimensions of a person's life, including the following needs: Spiritual, social, emotional, physical, sensory and intellectual.

A key aim is to provide opportunity to experience new things and to learn new skills to use in the future for a sustainable life with purpose and a broader work options.

"Unless the Lord builds the house, its builders labour in vain."
Psalm 127:1 (NIV)

SATURDAY BBQ

VISITORS WELCOME!

You are welcome to join us for our weekly BBQ, held every Saturday; rain, hail or shine.

- Come anytime from 3.00pm
- Dinner is at 6.00pm
- Spend the evening around the fire enjoying the company of others
- For the more adventurous; bring your climbing shoes, climb the cliff to view the Sherwood valley from above.
- Bring your own meat for the BBQ and something sweet to share
- We are an alcohol and smoke free facility.

Please contact us to arrange your visit,

Phone (02) 6649 2139

NEED HELP?

Know someone that needs help to overcome their addiction? Please don't hesitate to contact us!

www.ingramcontent.com/pod-product-compliance
Lightning Source LLC
Chambersburg PA
CBHW071922290426
44110CB00013B/1445